JAMES

JAMES

Biblical Commentary by

JOYCE MEYER

Faith
Words

NEW YORK   NASHVILLE

FaithWords
Hachette Book Group
1290 Avenue of the Americas, New York, NY 10104
faithwords.com
twitter.com/faithwords

First Edition: March 2019

FaithWords is a division of Hachette Book Group, Inc. The FaithWords name and logo are trademarks of Hachette Book Group, Inc.

The publisher is not responsible for websites (or their content) that are not owned by the publisher.

The Hachette Speakers Bureau provides a wide range of authors for speaking events. To find out more, go to www.hachettespeakersbureau.com or call (866) 376-6591.

Library of Congress Cataloging-in-Publication Data has been applied for.

ISBNs: 978-1-5460-2606-8 (hardcover), 978-1-5460-3532-9 (large print), 978-1-5460-2603-7 (ebook)

Printed in the United States of America

WOR

10 9 8 7 6 5 4 3 2 1

CONTENTS

ABOUT JAMES

Author: *James*
Date: *Approximately AD 48*
Audience: *Jewish Christians in the early church*

James was a common name in New Testament times, as it is today. Two of Jesus' twelve disciples were named James, but neither of them is the author of this letter. The author of this epistle is believed to be the James who is called the brother of Jesus, though he was technically his half brother. Jesus and James both had Mary as their mother; James's father was Joseph, while Jesus' Father was God Himself. Sometimes people do not see the greatness in their own family members because they are with those people all the time and they can see their flaws. Although James was the brother of Jesus, he recognized Him as the resurrected Lord, for he refers to himself as a servant of God and of the Lord Jesus Christ, which is very interesting and demonstrates James's humility because he could have easily written that he was the "brother" or relative of Jesus, but instead positions himself as a servant.

We can tell from the New Testament that James occupied a prominent place in the church in Jerusalem, and he is mentioned several times in the Book of Acts. In Acts 1:13–14, we see that James was one of the people praying in the Upper Room, along with Peter, John, Mary, and others. In Acts 12:17, after an angel released Peter from prison (Acts 12:6–10), Peter wanted to make sure James knew he was free, mentioning him by name. Along with Peter, James led what is known as the Jerusalem Council, which discussed the relationship between Gentile followers of Jesus and the law of Moses. James summarizes his judgment on the issues in Acts 15:13–21. When Paul returned to Jerusalem after some of his travels, he made a specific point to visit James (Acts 21:17–19), along with the elders of the church, to tell them what God was doing through his ministry. In Galatians, Paul mentions seeing James again, on a separate journey. Obviously, James had close relationships with Peter and Paul and was instrumental in the beginnings of the early church.

James's epistle has so much to say about living a successful Christian life and addresses a variety of topics important to growing Christians. This book teaches us not only that we need to read the Word of God and know what it says, but also that we need to act on it. According to H. A. Ironside, "The theme of the epistle is 'A Living Faith,' a faith that is evidenced by righteous living and godly behavior" (H. A. Ironside, *James and 1 and 2 Peter: An Ironside Expository Commentary* [Grand Rapids, MI: Kregel Publications, 1947; repr. 2008], 12). I like to describe "a living faith" as a faith that works and produces good things in our lives and in the lives of others.

One of the primary messages of this book is that true faith in God leads to good works. We serve God and do good works because of our genuine love for Him. There are all kinds of practical ways we can demonstrate our faith as we love God by loving other people—helping them, supporting them, encouraging them, and saying positive things to them and about them. We should always remember that good works do not prove that a person believes in God or has a relationship with Him, but that when we have faith in God, good works follow. Faith has to come first, because when good works are done in faith, God gets the glory.

There are five chapters in the Book of James, and H. A. Ironside describes them this way:

James 1: A Victorious Faith

James 2: A Manifested Faith

James 3: A Controlling and Energizing Faith

James 4: A Submissive Faith

James 5: A Patient and Expectant Faith

In five chapters, James covers many topics we need to understand as Christians. They include why tests and trials are important to the development of our faith and how we are to view them and endure them, wisdom, the importance of not being double-minded, persevering through challenges, resisting the devil, growing in faith, and praying effectively. In addition, James writes at length about the tongue, explaining how powerful our words can be. They can become dangerous to ourselves and to others when we use them carelessly, angrily, or without thinking, but they can bless and do good when we use them well.

The Book of James does not teach us much about specific doctrines of the Christian faith, as some epistles do, but offers us valuable lessons in practical Christian behavior and putting our faith into practice in the situations we face every day. For this reason, it is very important for us to read, study, and apply to our lives the truths and principles James provides for us. As you learn more about the Book of James, I pray that it will not only stir your faith in God but also inspire you to live righteously in practical ways and to do good works because of your love for Him and desire to glorify Him in your life.

Key Truths in James:

- Even in the face of trials, we can find joy because trials produce good fruit in our lives, the fruit of endurance leading to spiritual growth and maturity.
- Our words are extremely powerful, so watching our words and using them carefully is of the utmost importance. Negative words can bring pain and destruction, but positive words bring blessing.
- We can resist the devil and he will flee from us.
- Sincere, heartfelt prayers are very powerful and effective.

CHAPTER 1

◆—◀◆▶—◆

TESTS AND TRIALS LEAD TO JOY

The first chapter of James's epistle is a call to spiritual maturity. It addresses a variety of subjects important to the Christian life, including maintaining a good attitude through trials, avoiding double-mindedness, being content, accepting responsibility when we face temptation and letting it teach us something valuable, controlling our anger, obeying God's Word, carefully guarding our words, helping the poor, and being in the world without becoming like it.

Consider It Joy

James 1:2–4

*Consider it nothing but joy, my brothers and sisters, whenever you fall
into various trials. Be assured that the testing of your faith [through
experience] produces endurance [leading to spiritual maturity,
and inner peace]. And let endurance have its perfect result and do a
thorough work, so that you may be perfect and completely developed
[in your faith], lacking in nothing.*

James 1:2–4 addresses dealing with trials. James must have thought that
learning to behave properly in the midst of our trials is very important
since it is the first topic he addresses in this epistle. We don't always like to
think about the difficulties we face, but the Bible teaches us that they have
great value in our lives. We don't often *feel* joyous when facing difficulties,
but we can *consider* them to be so if we know what they produce in our lives
after they have done their work in us. People frequently tell me that their
trials have made them stronger and better than they were prior to them.

We can compare our trials and difficulties to a woman in labor. She feels
pain while delivering a child, yet she simultaneously feels joy because she
knows what the final outcome will be. Toward the end of her pregnancy, she
actually prays for her labor to begin. Even though she knows it will be difficult, she knows that the sooner it starts, the sooner she will have her baby.
She is ready to endure the hardship in order to reap the reward. We know that
the joy is greater than the pain, because in a couple of years many women
choose to endure all the pain again for the joy of having another child.

Just as a mother begins to long and even pray for her labor to start
because she does not want to be pregnant anymore, we can reach the
point where we are so tired of living the way we have been living—in
fear, anger, or jealousy; with our emotions up and down all the time;

struggling to make decisions instead of standing firm in faith—that
we are ready for something to help us get a breakthrough and move us
toward the next place of spiritual growth. Often, God uses trials to do
that. So if you are ready to leave your old ways of living behind, you can
pray, "God, let my labor begin." It may be painful for a while, but the joy
that will ultimately come to you will be worth it.

During times of trial we grow spiritually, and we become stronger. Trials also develop the character of Christ in us and bring out of us endurance,
steadfastness, and patience, which are all powerful qualities that Jesus displayed and that we should deeply desire. No matter what we face, God will
always work it out for our good if we go through it with the right attitude.

Embracing difficulty, rather than despising it, is challenging for most
of us. We tend to resist it, struggle against it, and look for some way to get
out of it. Although this is a natural response, it is not the best one. The
better thing to do is pray that you can endure whatever comes with good
temper, trust God to deliver you at the right time, and believe that He will
cause good to come out of it. It may help you to tell God exactly how you
feel about what you are going through and also voice your trust in Him.
God is good, and we can be assured that whatever happens to us will
work out for our good and help us grow spiritually if we will let it.

Our attitude during times of trials and difficulties plays a part in
determining how long they will last and what we will get from them. We
can waste our pain, or we can let it become our gain.

If you believe God is always working for your good—even through
tough times—the day will come when you will be very glad you stopped
resisting and running from difficulties and learned how to walk through
them with God, all the way to victory. God will not leave you stuck in your
troubles. You are going *through* them, and you will have a great testimony
and be able to help others through their struggles when you get to the
other side. We all want a testimony, but we should remember that the word
begins with *test*! Without the test, there will never be a good testimony.

Let me encourage you to always focus on the strength you are gaining
rather than the opposition you are facing. Let the trouble you encounter be an opportunity to exercise your faith, and that faith will become

stronger. The stronger our faith is, the less any kind of trouble bothers us. We need to be able to say with the apostle Paul, "I know what it is to be in need, and I know what it is to have plenty. I have learned the secret of being content in any and every situation, whether well fed or hungry, whether living in plenty or in want. I can do all this through him who gives me strength" (Phil. 4:12–13 NIV).

Personal Reflection

Even when circumstances are very difficult for you, do you believe that God is working for your good?

_____

_____

_____

_____

_____

_____

_____

_____

_____

_____

_____

_____

The Amplified Classic version of Isaiah 41:10 says, "Fear not [there is nothing to fear], for I am with you; do not look around you in terror *and* be dismayed, for I am your God. I will strengthen *and* harden you to difficulties, yes, I will help you; yes, I will hold you up *and* retain you with My [victorious] right hand of rightness *and* justice." If God Himself strengthens us and hardens us to difficulties, the trials that upset us now will not bother us again in the future. Every time one trial hardens us, we can bear the next one with greater strength.

Also in Isaiah 41, verse 15 says, "Behold, I will make you to be a new, sharp, threshing instrument which has teeth; you shall thresh the mountains and beat them small, and shall make the hills like chaff" (AMPC). This verse teaches us that God wants us to grow up. Spiritual babies need spiritual milk, but as we grow spiritually, He wants to give us "meat"— and we will need to be like a "sharp, threshing instrument which has teeth" in order to handle it. Trials help us grow out of spiritual infancy toward spiritual maturity. God will never give us more than we can bear, but He will try to help us grow.

One thing God wants to do in us when we go through trials is teach us to take our eyes off of ourselves and focus instead on what we can do for other people and for Him. Isaiah 41:17 says, "The poor and needy are seeking water when there is none; their tongues are parched with thirst. I the Lord will answer them; I, the God of Israel, will not forsake them" (AMPC). The difficulties we face help us grow and become vessels fit for God's use, so He can work through us to help other people.

The first word of James 1:2 is *consider,* and it is such an important word that we need to look closely at it. Considering something is related to our thought process about it, so this one word teaches us a lot about reaching the point where our trials and tests become a source of joy to us. If we can train our minds to think of trials as seeds that will ultimately bring a harvest of joy, we'll be on our way to experiencing the joy they can bring to our lives. According to James 1:3–4, trials produce endurance, spiritual maturity, and inner peace, so we are "completely developed" in our faith, lacking nothing. These are all powerful character traits that

Jesus displayed and that we should deeply desire. They enable us to reach our goals and live in God's plan for our lives. They all carry the idea that we need the ability to go through difficult things trusting God, allowing Him to do in us the work that needs to be done, without giving up.

Although trials ultimately work good things in us, they often bring bad things out of us first. They cause things like anger, fear, jealousy, complaining, volatile emotions, and negative thoughts and speech to surface, helping us face them and letting God deal with them and set us free from them. If we will continue to walk with God all the way through our trials, we will see the good fruit He wants to develop in our lives. I often say that our trials are just tests, and we should pass them quickly—or we will just get to keep taking them over and over again until we do.

God wants to bless us—more than we can imagine. But He cannot bless us in the natural realm beyond where we are spiritually. We would not give a three-year-old the keys to our car because we know he cannot handle an automobile. We keep the keys away from him, even if he wants to drive the car, because we love him and we would never put him in danger. Similarly, God will not give us things He knows we are not mature enough to handle properly. I often pray, "God, please do not give me anything I cannot handle and still keep You first in my life." In order to be good stewards of all He wants to bless us with, we need to be mature—and that's where trials and tests come in. They develop maturity and character in us, which is why James says we can think about them as "nothing but joy."

Always remember that each time you go through a difficulty in a mature manner, you grow stronger and stronger. Soon the trials you encounter in life won't upset you as they once did because you know they won't last forever and that God will work something good out of them.

While we do not like going through difficulties, it is important for us to understand that trials are not evidence of God's displeasure or anger. He does not allow or use them in our lives to punish us, but to help us grow. As we learn to think rightly about our trials, let's remember these three key points:

1. If we profess to have faith, we can be guaranteed that sooner or later our faith will be put to the test.
2. Although we may open doors for the enemy through sin and disobedience, God will still use our trials for our good and advancement, as we trust Him.
3. The last thing we need during times of trials is condemnation on top of the difficulties we already have to deal with.

Knowing these things will help us stand against the lie that, when we face difficulties, God is punishing us for some sin we have committed.

There are several ways trials help us:

1. They train us. They force us to use our faith, which enables us to eventually become stable during the storms of life.
2. They humble us (see Prov. 18:12; 2 Cor. 12:7; 1 Pet. 5:6–8). Nothing humbles us more than finding ourselves in the midst of a situation or crisis we cannot handle and having to look to God and to other people for help.
3. They remind us to be totally dependent on God (2 Cor. 1:8–9).
4. They help us develop character (Rom. 5:3–4).
5. For the glory of God, our trials give us a testimony (Ps. 40:4–5; 71:14–17; Rev. 12:11).

Trials also produce patience in us. In fact, the Amplified Classic version of James 1:4 says, "But let endurance and steadfastness *and* patience have full play and do a thorough work, so that you may be [people] perfectly and fully developed [with no defects], lacking in nothing." Other translations, such as the King James Version and the New King James Version, also use the word *patience* in this verse.

When people are fully patient, they are complete and "fully developed, lacking in nothing." That is amazing to me, and it teaches us that patience has great power. When we become fully patient, we are able to trust God for His timing and His way and we are convinced He knows exactly how to take care of our problems and do what we have asked, if it is according to His will. We are able to dwell in peace and enjoy our lives even in times of trial and tribulation.

When you were born again, the nature of God was deposited in you. Patience is part of that nature, so it is in you—even though it may be just a tiny seed right now—and God will work with you to develop it so you can experience the blessings of being fully patient.

I personally had to take quite a journey to develop patience. I have said that a lot had to be worked out of me before I experienced any patience. It was buried in my spirit, deposited there by the Holy Spirit, but it was underneath my carnal soul. Thank God that He is patient with us! The Holy Spirit helped me and taught me until I learned the value of being patient, and He will do the same for you. I have not arrived at perfect patience, but I am continuing to make progress.

In Psalm 31:1–3, David gives us a picture of patience exemplified:

In You, O Lord, do I put my trust *and* seek refuge; let me never be put to shame *or* [have my hope in You] disappointed; deliver me in Your righteousness! Bow down Your ear to me, deliver me speedily! Be my Rock of refuge, a strong Fortress to save me! Yes, You are my Rock and my Fortress; therefore for Your name's sake lead me and guide me. (AMPC)

As we grow in patience, strong Christian character is developed. We no longer crave what God sees fit to withhold, and we are content with His timing in our lives. We trust God's Word and believe Romans 8:28—that God is working all things together for our good—and we enter God's rest.

Much can be said about trials and their benefits and what we need to learn through them. But let me end this section by saying that we will have various trials and tribulations throughout our lives. Our goal should be to navigate them well and get through them as quickly as the Lord allows.

Personal Reflection

How have tests and trials strengthened your faith or caused
you to grow spiritually?

_____

_____

_____

_____

_____

_____

_____

_____

_____

_____

_____

_____

_____

_____

_____

_____

_____

_____

_____

_____

CHAPTER 2

ASKING IN FAITH, CONTENTMENT, AND PERSEVERANCE

When You Need Wisdom

James 1:5

*If any of you lacks wisdom [to guide him through a decision or
circumstance], he is to ask of [our benevolent] God, who gives to
everyone generously and without rebuke or blame, and it will be
given to him.*

One of the most beneficial things we can seek in life is wisdom. When
we use wisdom, we make decisions now that we will be happy with later.
When we follow God's wisdom, it will always lead us to His best for us,
and it will help us not to live in regret.

When we find ourselves needing wisdom in some area of our lives,
we have two choices: We can handle the situation the natural way or the
spiritual way. James 1:5 teaches us how to solve any type of dilemma
the spiritual way. It says that when we don't have the wisdom we need,
we should simply ask God what to do.

We may not receive an answer immediately, but we will find that
divine wisdom (wisdom beyond our natural understanding) will begin
to operate through us, helping us know what to do. As this verse promises, not only will God give us the wisdom we need, but He will give it
generously.

Personal Reflection

In what situations do you need God's wisdom right now?

_____

_____

_____

_____

_____

_____

_____

_____

_____

_____

Doubt and Double-Mindedness

James 1:6–8

But he must ask [for wisdom] in faith, without doubting [God's willingness to help], for the one who doubts is like a billowing surge of the sea that is blown about and tossed by the wind. For such a person ought not to think or expect that he will receive anything [at all] from the Lord, being a double-minded man, unstable and restless in all his ways [in everything he thinks, feels, or decides].

When we face trials, we can ask for God's help with the confident assurance that we will receive it. Even if we have contributed to our troubles, God is always ready to help us. He will not hold our mistakes against us or remind us of them. This is amazing love!

It is vital to our spiritual growth that we determine to believe God at all times—not to believe for a little while, then fall into doubt. Not to believe for a month and then stop believing. This wavering between faith and doubt is called double-mindedness, and James teaches us that the double-minded person should not expect to receive anything from God because he is "unstable and restless in all his ways."

One of my favorite Scriptures is Mark 5:35–36, which is the story of Jairus, a ruler of the synagogue, and his daughter. Jesus was on His way to Jairus's house to pray for his sick daughter when someone interrupted Him, delaying His journey. While Jesus was talking to that person, someone came to tell Jairus that his daughter had died and suggested that he not bother Jesus anymore. In other words, it was too late. Jesus didn't get there in time.

The passage says that Jesus overheard these comments but ignored them. And He encouraged Jairus to "keep on believing." After that, He raised Jairus's daughter from the dead. We need to do exactly what Jairus did. When the enemy tempts us to doubt, we may hear the temptation, but we can choose to ignore it—and keep on believing.

We will all be tempted to doubt at times, because we have an enemy who always wants to pull us away from God and keep us from obeying God's Word. According to John 10:10, the enemy does nothing but "steal and kill and destroy," and he wants us to help him do it by giving in to temptation. But *feeling* temptation does not mean we have to surrender to it. Through God's strength, we can resist our enemy.

Also in John 10:10, Jesus says that He came so we could "have and enjoy life, and have it in abundance [to the full, till it overflows]." If we focus on ourselves or on our circumstances, doubt gains ground in our minds. The story of Peter walking on water teaches us to focus not on what is going on around us, but on Jesus. When he focused on the wind and the waves, he began to sink (Matt. 14:28–31). But as soon as he looked at Jesus instead of his surroundings, a miracle happened, and he was able to walk across the sea. If we will be like Peter and keep our eyes on Jesus, we can be firm in faith and enjoy the abundant life He died to give us.

Jesus frequently encouraged people to be strong in faith, and He actually rebuked doubt in Mark 4:35–40, when a strong storm arose on the sea of Galilee and He was sleeping in the boat. The disciples grew fearful and began to doubt that He cared about them. He responded, "Why are you afraid? Do you still have no faith and confidence [in Me]?" (Mark 4:40).

I have said for years that we need to doubt our doubts. We are to stand strong in faith, not always knowing exactly what God will do or when He will do it, but believing He will always do what is best for us at the proper time.

Pray without Doubt

If we pray without doubt, we will receive. Mark 11:22–24 says:

> Jesus replied, "Have faith in God [constantly]. I assure you *and* most solemnly say to you, whoever says to this mountain, 'Be lifted up and thrown into the sea!' and does not doubt in his heart [in God's unlimited power], but believes that what he says is going

to take place, it will be done for him [in accordance with God's will]. For this reason I am telling you, whatever things you ask for in prayer [in accordance with God's will], believe [with confident trust] that you have received them, and they will be *given* to you."

When we pray, we need to be sure to the best of our ability that what we are asking for is the will of God. We also need to keep our eyes on Jesus so that circumstances or delays in answered prayer do not distract us from our faith, causing us to doubt (Heb. 12:2).

If we ask God for something—the right thing at the right time according to His will—and we are spiritually mature enough to handle it, and we ask in Jesus' name (presenting all that He is, not who we are), He will do it. We can count on this, because God is not a man that He should lie (Num. 23:19). He keeps His promises.

Make Decisions without Doubt

One way doubt can hurt us is in the area of making decisions. When we have prayed and thoughtfully made a decision, we need to stick with it. Colossians 3:2 says to "Set your mind *and* keep focused *habitually* on the things above [the heavenly things], not on things that are on the earth [which have only temporal value]." Once we decide what to do in a situation, we need to keep that decision set in our minds, not doubting it, and move forward.

A lot of our doubts come from insecurity and a lack of confidence, or from fear that we will be wrong about something. God wants us to trust Him to help us with our decisions and to be confident in Him. We will all be wrong at times, but God will help us get back on the right track, and He will use our mistakes to help us learn something if we will keep trusting Him.

Eight steps to a solid decision are:

1. Pray.
2. Consider all your options.
3. Write down the advantages and disadvantages of each option.
4. Make a choice.

5. Don't try to make an important decision when you are emotional, because it probably won't be a good one.
6. Sleep on the decision. See if you have peace the next morning.
7. If you feel you need confirmation about the decision, check with a mature, trusted Christian professional or friend.
8. Start taking action.

Be Content

James 1:9–11

Let the brother in humble circumstances glory in his high position [as a born-again believer, called to the true riches and to be an heir of God]; and the rich man is to glory in being humbled [by trials revealing human frailty, knowing true riches are found in the grace of God], for like the flower of the grass he will pass away. For the sun rises with a scorching wind and withers the grass; its flower falls off and its beauty fades away; so too will the rich man, in the midst of his pursuits, fade away.

No matter how rich people are in material goods, they are actually poverty-stricken unless they are rich in their relationship with the Lord. In the same way, no matter how poor people may be in material goods, they are wealthy if they know the Lord and understand His love for them. Keeping God first in our lives is the most important thing we can do.

Circumstances in our lives can change quickly, just as a flower may bloom and then in a few days be wilted. This should not frighten us, because as long as we have Jesus, we have the most valuable thing we can ever have. We should never let our circumstances dictate our joy; they are always fluctuating, but God remains the same.

Whether we have a little or a lot, we can be content, and contentment is a significant aspect of spiritual maturity. Paul said, "I have learned to be content [and self-sufficient through Christ, satisfied to the point where I am not disturbed or uneasy] regardless of my circumstances" (Phil. 4:11). He knew how to live with meager provision and in prosperity (Phil. 4:12), and we would be wise to follow his example.

To be content does not mean that we never desire change or better circumstances, but it does mean that while we are waiting for God to do the things that need to be done in our lives, we can be happy and content with the life He is providing for us right now.

No matter what you don't have, always be thankful for the things you do have. Doing this will keep you from getting discouraged and being discontented.

Personal Reflection

Whether you consider yourself a person who has a little or a lot, are you keeping God first in your life? If not, what changes can you make to straighten out your priorities?

_____

_____

_____

_____

_____

_____

_____

_____

_____

_____

_____

_____

Steadfastness and Perseverance
James 1:12

Blessed [happy, spiritually prosperous, favored by God] is the man who is steadfast under trial and perseveres when tempted; for when he has passed the test and been approved, he will receive the [victor's] crown of life which the Lord has promised to those who love Him.

James offers an encouraging promise to those who are steadfast—patient and stable—when facing difficulties and who can persevere through temptation. These believers will receive the victor's crown of life.

Steadfast faithfulness that perseveres and overcomes temptation is a powerful thing! We all enjoy having a good testimony, but it is interesting to note that the word *testimony* begins with *test*. God rewards those who persevere and don't give up in hard times. If we can keep that in mind, we can better endure the hardships we experience on earth.

CHAPTER 3

DEALING WITH TEMPTATION AND BEING A DOER OF THE WORD

A Proper Response to Temptation

James 1:13–15

Let no one say when he is tempted, "I am being tempted by God" [for temptation does not originate from God, but from our own flaws]; for God cannot be tempted by [what is] evil, and He Himself tempts no one. But each one is tempted when he is dragged away, enticed and baited [to commit sin] by his own [worldly] desire (lust, passion). Then when the illicit desire has conceived, it gives birth to sin; and when sin has run its course, it gives birth to death.

It's important to understand that temptation comes to everyone and it often happens during times of trial, when we may be stressed, tired, distracted, or vulnerable in some other way. God will allow us to be tested, but He will never tempt us to sin. However, Satan will, just as he tempted Jesus in the wilderness (Luke 4:1–13). When we are tempted, we need to recognize that God wants to give us the strength to overcome the temptation and grow in our faith.

We succumb to temptation when we have evil desires, lusts, or passions that are not being controlled, or in other areas of personal weakness. I am never tempted to steal—that is not a weakness for me. However, I am frequently tempted to become impatient when things are not going the way they should be—that is a weakness for me, so that's how the enemy is likely to tempt me. I don't see the tendency to become impatient unless I am under some kind of trial. When everything in life is going great, I am not impatient at all. This is one reason trials are good for us. They reveal our weaknesses to us so we can pray about them and ask the Holy Spirit to strengthen us. When we see our weaknesses, we no longer blame others for our problems.

We should take responsibility for our behavior and allow the Lord to help us. Blaming others is often just a way of avoiding taking personal responsibility for our mistakes. I once heard someone say that the first step toward personal healing and wholeness is to take 100 percent responsibility for your life. I believe this because for years, I thought everything that happened was someone else's fault. I made no progress

Personal Reflection

Are you praying that you will stand firm against the temptations you face?

_____

_____

_____

_____

_____

_____

_____

_____

_____

_____

_____

until I started taking responsibility for the part that I played in my problems. Even if our problems are not our fault, the attitudes we have toward them are our responsibility. We can't control what other people do, but we can control how we respond to them and to their actions.

Learning to handle things responsibly is an important step toward turning tragedy into triumph. God is greater than anything that can happen to us and anything anyone can do to us. He will use things we may view as negative to make us better and stronger.

It is pointless to pray that we won't be tempted, but we can and should pray that we will stand strong against temptation. Jesus says in Matthew 26:41, "Keep *actively* watching and praying that you may not come into temptation; the spirit is willing, but the body is weak."

God Is Always Good

James 1:17–18

*Every good thing given and every perfect gift is from above; it comes
down from the Father of lights [the Creator and Sustainer of the
heavens], in whom there is no variation [no rising or setting] or
shadow cast by His turning [for He is perfect and never changes]. It
was of His own will that He gave us birth [as His children] by
the word of truth, so that we would be a kind of first fruits of His
creatures [a prime example of what He created to be set apart to
Himself—sanctified, made holy for His divine purposes].*

James uses these few sentences to remind us that God is *always* and *only*
good. One of the most detrimental things we can do is blame God when
we experience pain, loss, or unjust treatment. Neither should we blame
Him when we end up in situations that tempt us. These things are all part
of everyone's life, and keeping in mind that God is always good and that
He is our Helper and Friend is the best attitude we can have.

Doers of the Word

James 1:19–20

Understand this, my beloved brothers and sisters. Let everyone
be quick to hear [be a careful, thoughtful listener], slow to speak
[a speaker of carefully chosen words and], slow to anger [patient,
reflective, forgiving]; for the [resentful, deep-seated] anger of man does
not produce the righteousness of God [that standard of behavior which
He requires from us].

Mature Christians are quick to hear, slow to speak, and slow to get angry. Anytime I see a list such as this one in the Bible, I like to ask myself how I am doing. Am I quick to hear, slow to speak, and slow to become angry? I can say that I am usually slow to become angry, but sometimes I am not as quick to hear or slow to speak as I would like to be. I have improved over the years, but I am certainly not where I need and want to be. I encourage you not to ever think, *I'm doing good enough.* A desire to continually grow in godliness is a good desire and one that God admires and honors. Like Paul, let's press toward the mark of perfection without feeling condemned about our mistakes (Phil. 3:13–14).

Over the years I have realized that being quick to hear—in other words, to listen to others more—is very beneficial. We can learn a lot by listening carefully and patiently to other people. I believe this verse encourages us to do that, but I believe it also carries another meaning and applies to listening to the Holy Spirit in the midst of situations so we can respond to them well.

We live in two worlds: the world we can see and the world we can't. We exist in the physical realm, but there is also a spiritual aspect to our lives. We can be involved in a conversation with someone and be quick to hear that person, but we can also have an ear turned toward God. As we interact with other people, we can be listening for God to guide us, asking Him, "What do I say now? Should I say anything about what she just said, or should I be quiet?" Taking time to seek and hear from God— even quickly, in the midst of a conversation—before we speak can be very wise.

Jesus was always listening to God in the midst of His activity. At times when He was falsely accused, He frequently didn't even answer His accusers. One time I believe He was listening to God intently was when He encountered the woman caught in adultery (John 8:1–11). He knew she had broken the law, and He knew the Pharisees were trying to get Him to break the law, too. According to the law, her punishment would have been stoning. Instead of condemning her, He simply asked each person around her who was without sin to throw the first stone at her. One by one, they put down their stones and walked away. If we would be like Jesus, slow down, hear from God, and take more time before we speak, things would be much better.

Hear and Obey

James 1:21–25

So get rid of all uncleanness and all that remains of wickedness, and with a humble spirit receive the word [of God] which is implanted [actually rooted in your heart], which is able to save your souls. But prove yourselves doers of the word [actively and continually obeying God's precepts], and not merely listeners [who hear the word but fail to internalize its meaning], deluding yourselves [by unsound reasoning contrary to the truth]. For if anyone only listens to the word without obeying it, he is like a man who looks very carefully at his natural face in a mirror; for once he has looked at himself and gone away, he immediately forgets what he looked like. But he who looks carefully into the perfect law, the law of liberty, and faithfully abides by it, not having become a [careless] listener who forgets but an active doer [who obeys], he will be blessed and favored by God in what he does [in his life of obedience].

James immediately follows his instruction to be quick to hear, slow to speak, and slow to anger with encouragement to receive the Word of God with humility. It's almost as though James first says, "Here's what you do" and then says, "Here's how you do it."

God's Word has power to change us if we receive it with meekness and with a humble spirit. It saves (matures) the souls of those who are born again, and when received with a humble heart, it actually has the power to cleanse us from evil things like anger, selfishness, and being undisciplined. It gives us the strength to recognize and act on what God wants us to do.

I like to think of God's Word as a huge medicine cabinet. It contains everything we need to solve every problem we have. Just as we can be sick or in pain, and then be healed after we take a certain medication regularly over a period of time, if we will read, study, and obey the Word regularly, it will take care of the things that trouble our souls.

If you need help with a particular struggle in your life—perhaps jealousy, anger, sadness, selfishness, fear, or something else—help is available in God's Word. Simply look up Scriptures pertaining to that topic and read what the Word says about it; speak those verses aloud, meditate on them, and obey them—and the power of the Word will heal your soul.

Personal Reflection

Pray and ask God to show you any areas of your life that don't line up with His Word. What changes do you need to make to live in obedience to His ways and plan for you?

_____

_____

_____

_____

_____

_____

_____

_____

_____

_____

_____

We can go to church three times each week, watch Christian television each morning, and hear Bible teachings in the car as we commute to work, but if we never do anything with what we hear, it won't do us any good. This is why it is so important that we both hear and obey. We are blessed as we live a life of obedience, not just a life of hearing or knowing.

If we merely listen and don't obey, James 1:22 says we delude ourselves by "unsound reasoning," meaning we find a reason to be exempt from obeying. As an example, let's say that I notice someone on my staff and feel in my heart that she could use a blessing. Then let's say I notice a bracelet on my wrist and remember that the woman complimented it earlier that day. If God leads me to give it to her because she needs a blessing but I want to keep it, I could come up with all kinds of reasons not to give it to her. Maybe I think she would like it, but it wouldn't look good with the outfit she is wearing that day. Maybe I reason that it wouldn't fit her, or I think, *I have never seen her wear a bracelet before. I don't think she even likes bracelets!* All of those reasons could talk me out of obeying the God-given impulse to give her the bracelet. If I listen to them, I delude myself and end up not obeying what God led me to do.

True Religion

James 1:26–27

If anyone thinks himself to be religious [scrupulously observant of the rituals of his faith], and does not control his tongue but deludes his own heart, this person's religion is worthless (futile, barren). Pure and unblemished religion [as it is expressed in outward acts] in the sight of our God and Father is this: to visit and look after the fatherless and the widows in their distress, and to keep oneself uncontaminated by the [secular] world.

Being able to control your tongue is an important part of spiritual maturity. The Book of James deals with this subject extensively, and I will address it in greater detail later in this book. Here, I want to simply say this: *If you want to locate yourself, listen to yourself.* This means that we can judge our level of spiritual maturity and see where we are with God by simply listening to ourselves—to what we say about God, about others, and about ourselves. Our words are verbal expressions of our souls, and we can tell what is in us by hearing what comes out of us. If we cannot control what we say, James teaches that our religion is worthless.

In contrast to worthless religion, James says the expression of "pure and unblemished religion" may be seen in acts of mercy toward the poor. We don't go to church or to a Bible study and then go home and do nothing; we demonstrate our love for God in practical ways. Instruction about our responsibility to the poor is found throughout the Word of God. The way we treat them reveals the true condition of our heart. Job 31:16–22, written long before James, expresses the same truth:

If I have withheld from the poor what *they* desired, or have caused the eyes of the widow to look in vain [for relief], or have eaten my morsel [of food] alone, and did not share it with the orphan (but from my youth the orphan grew up with me as with a father, and from my mother's womb I have been the widow's guide), if I have seen anyone perish for lack of clothing, or any poor person without covering, if his loins have not thanked *and* blessed me [for clothing them], and if he was not warmed with the fleece of my sheep, if I have lifted my hand against the orphan, because I saw [that the judges would be] my help at the [council] gate, then let my shoulder fall away from its socket, and my arm be broken off at the elbow.

Personal Reflection

What can you do to help the poor, orphans, or widows?

_____

_____

_____

_____

_____

_____

_____

_____

_____

_____

_____

Finally, James 1:27 says that the proof of our true religion is to keep ourselves "uncontaminated by the [secular] world." We often hear that we are to be "in" the world but not "of" the world. This means we can enjoy the good things the world offers, but it is important for us not to grow too attached to them or allow them to pollute our hearts and minds. God's Word says that we are to live in the world as strangers and aliens, and to remember that we are simply passing through. This world is not our home. God is our home, and our journey through this world will ultimately lead us to live in His presence for eternity.

As Christians it is so important for us to live in the world as good ambassadors and examples for Christ, yet to keep ourselves from becoming like the world. Part of being able to do that successfully involves having one ear tuned to God as we go about our daily lives, listening to Him, making quick adjustments as He leads us, and acting on what we've heard.

CHAPTER 4

LIVING BY THE ROYAL LAW OF LOVE

The second chapter of James is divided into two parts: verses 1-13, which I will address in this chapter, and verses 14-26, which I will write about in chapter 5. The first part of it stresses the importance of not thinking that we can be justified or made righteous before God by keeping the Law of Moses, which is the law of the Old Testament. Because we are New Testament believers, we do not live under the Law of Moses, but under a new law. It is called the Royal Law of Liberty, and it is basically the law of love.

As New Covenant believers, we now live not under the law of rituals but the law of love. When we walk in love, we will keep all the other commandments. In my opinion, we need to increase our focus on loving God and loving others as we love ourselves. Jesus said that if we love Him, we will obey Him (John 14:15), and simple obedience to God solves all of our problems. We should love and respect ourselves because God loves us, and we should love others, being more concerned with their welfare than our own. A person may strive to follow all the laws (rules and regulations) found in the Bible and still not walk in love.

Treating Everyone the Same

James 2:1–7

My fellow believers, do not practice your faith in our glorious Lord Jesus Christ with an attitude of partiality [toward people—show no favoritism, no prejudice, no snobbery]. For if a man comes into your meeting place wearing a gold ring and fine clothes, and a poor man in dirty clothes also comes in, and you pay special attention to the one who wears the fine clothes, and say to him, "You sit here in this good seat," and you tell the poor man, "You stand over there, or sit down [on the floor] by my footstool," have you not discriminated among yourselves, and become judges with wrong motives? Listen, my beloved brothers and sisters: has not God chosen the poor of this world to be rich in faith and [as believers to be] heirs of the kingdom which He promised to those who love Him? But you [in contrast] have dishonored the poor man. Is it not the rich who oppress and exploit you, and personally drag you into the courts of law? Do they not blaspheme the precious name [of Christ] by which you are called?

In these verses, James warns us repeatedly to treat all people the same way, regardless of their wealth or social standing. The selfishness of the human heart is easily seen when we are inclined to favor the wealthy or those we consider influential or powerful, while ignoring the poor and those who cannot do anything for us.

The importance of valuing other people can be seen throughout history. Wars have been fought for centuries simply because people from one culture or ethnic background despised people from another.

- This kind of conflict began in Genesis, when Cain killed Abel because he hated him.

- From 1618 to 1648, Catholics and Protestants fought a war based on religious hatred.
- During the Holocaust, six million people were killed because of their Jewish faith.
- From 1967 to 1970, one million people died in a Nigerian civil war between two tribes who hated each other.
- During the Rwandan Genocide, over a period of only one hundred days from April to July 1994, a million people were brutally slaughtered as a result of fighting between the Tutsi tribe and the Hutu tribe—because of their hatred for one another.
- In Ireland, fighting has raged for years because of conflict between Catholics and Protestants.
- There is also a war that has lasted more than 960 years between the Western Catholic Church based in Rome and the Eastern Catholic Church (Greek or Russian Orthodox). The two groups split in 1054 and have not fellowshipped together officially since that time. Their fighting is rooted in a doctrinal difference over the origin of the Holy Spirit and whether they should celebrate the Eucharist with leavened or unleavened bread.

And we wonder why we as Christians struggle to influence the world for Christ!

As you can see, differences between people or groups can lead to great trouble and heartbreak. Even today, other arguments and prejudices are rampant among Christians. There are literally thousands of denominations and groups that distinguish themselves from others based on a certain principle or idea, or on the way they interpret Scripture. This is hurting the cause of the gospel, and I am sure it is not pleasing to God.

If we want to live by God's Word, we need to ask ourselves if we can fellowship with other Christians who may not believe exactly as we do on every point of theology, or who are not part of our denomination. Can we refrain from judging them and love them as the Bible teaches us? Can we be friends with people from different socioeconomic backgrounds? Can we stop looking at the color of a person's skin and simply see a human being? I hope so.

I am not recommending that we become so inclusive that we accept sin without confronting it, nor am I suggesting that we ignore and never deal with doctrinal error, but we can certainly love all kinds of people and demonstrate basic human kindness to all. If we do disagree, we can learn to disagree agreeably and respectfully.

James calls special attention to relationships between the rich and the poor. When he writes about those who are "rich in faith," I think about qualities I have noticed in people who lack material wealth but trust and follow God wholeheartedly. Very often they are kind and ready to help others in need. They are generous and willing to sacrifice for others. They value and show more appreciation for the little that they do have than many people who live in abundance.

Dave and I, along with our team, have often traveled to third world countries where poverty is prevalent. The people in those places have offered us more genuine Christian hospitality than I have ever seen in wealthy parts of the United States. I have concluded that these people typically place value on what is truly valuable—other people and relationships—instead of on money or material goods. They have not had an excess of material things, so they have never made those things more important than they should be.

James clearly understood that everyone is important and that God sees all people equally, loving us all the same. As we grow in our walk with God, we also need to value and esteem everyone: not look down on some or show favoritism to others.

There are all kinds of differences that exist among people. Perhaps the most obvious differences are in the way people look. We encounter that difference every day. Years ago, if you walked into a shop or a church or an office building—even if you stepped onto an airplane for a flight—people dressed a certain way. They usually wore what we termed their "dress clothes" and were typically neat, with their clothes pressed, and they would not have even considered wearing something with holes in it. Their hair was almost always their natural color or dyed to match it. The only piercings we saw were for ladies' earrings, and tattoos were rarely seen in public.

Personal Reflection

Do you need to broaden your circle of inclusion and learn to value people who are different from you?

_____

_____

_____

_____

_____

_____

_____

_____

_____

_____

_____

_____

_____

Today, some people look different. They wear clothes with wrinkles and holes—and they are considered stylish in today's culture! They may have streaks of pink, purple, or blue running through their hair, or a complete green, purple, or pink hairstyle. I see piercings in lots of places, and tattoos that sometimes cover almost all of a person's arms and legs.

If people in my generation—perhaps those age fifty and older—are not careful, we can judge and criticize the young ones who do not look like we do. We may look down on them and form opinions about them that are completely wrong, based on their outward appearance. At the same time, young people may look at older ones and decide that we have nothing in common with them and are not worth talking to. The truth is, God loves everyone and all kinds of people love God. If a person wears something I would never wear, it does not eliminate the anointing (the power and presence of God) in his or her life. But if I have a snooty, "I'm better than you" attitude, that condemnation *will* have a negative effect on the anointing of my life.

Critical judgment of other people is a huge problem in the world and among Christians, and each of us needs to take a good, long look at our own attitude to make sure it is not a problem for us. Being judgmental is the fruit of pride, and I think pride is the worst of all sins. It was because of pride that Satan fell from heaven, and the Bible says that pride always comes before a fall or destruction (Proverbs 16:18). Let us pray that we always walk in love and treat all people as valuable because they are very valuable to God.

If we can obey James's instruction and refuse to show partiality, it will be very pleasing to God, and I believe it will increase the power of the Holy Spirit in our lives. We can learn from each other and appreciate our differences as we grow in showing God's love to one another.

The Royal Law

James 2:8–9

If, however, you are [really] fulfilling the royal law according to the Scripture, "You shall love your neighbor as yourself [that is, if you have an unselfish concern for others and do things for their benefit]" you are doing well. But if you show partiality [prejudice, favoritism], you are committing sin and are convicted by the Law as offenders.

The Royal Law is the law of loving others as we love ourselves. This is exactly what Jesus was talking about in John 13:34–35: "I am giving you a new commandment, that you love one another. Just as I have loved you, so you too are to love one another. By this everyone will know that you are My disciples, if you have love *and* unselfish concern for one another." He also spoke of it in Matthew 22:37–39, when His disciples asked Him what was the greatest commandment in the Law. He said: " 'You shall love the Lord your God with all your heart, and with all your soul, and with all your mind.' This is the first and greatest commandment. The second is like it, 'You shall love your neighbor as yourself [that is, unselfishly seek the best or higher good for others].' "

Love is seen in the way we treat people. Those we encounter may not remember what we say to them, but they will remember how we make them feel. When they think about their interactions with us, they will remember whether we made them feel good or bad, valuable or worthless. We can do all kinds of small things that help people feel good about themselves and communicate that they have value—anything from truly listening to people and not interrupting them while they speak, to letting them know that we truly enjoy being around them and are glad to have them in our lives, to giving them some type of gift or meeting a need they may have. We can speak to someone standing alone in a crowded room or say "thank you" to the janitor who cleans our office or the person who delivers the mail.

I believe that, to God, loving other people and treating them well is one of the most important things we can do. If we spend our lives loving people, valuing them, and treating them well, we will be blessed. I have never seen a selfish, self-centered person who was truly happy.

Breaking One Law Means Breaking Them All
James 2:10–13

For whoever keeps the whole Law but stumbles in one point, *he has become guilty of [breaking] all of it. For He who said, "Do not commit adultery," also said, "Do not murder." Now if you do not commit adultery, but you murder, you have become guilty of transgressing the [entire] Law. Speak and act [consistently] as people who are going to be judged by the law of liberty [that moral law that frees obedient Christians from the bondage of sin]. For judgment will be merciless to one who has shown no mercy; but [to the one who has shown mercy] mercy triumphs [victoriously] over judgment.*

If we try to live under the Old Covenant law, it's like playing a game of Whac-a-Mole (a game for children in which a hammer is used to whack a wooden mole that sticks his head out of a hole, but as soon as that mole is whacked, another one pops up). We may be able to keep one law, but if we break one, we are guilty of breaking them all. That is exhausting and leads to a miserable life. There is no way to keep every single law, and when we are in Christ, we are no longer bound to the old laws—we can live under the new law of love. Loving God and others releases joy in our lives more than anything else I know.

We should be careful not to let anyone put us under any law except the law of love. For example, we don't need to observe religious rituals while ignoring other people and failing to show them love and kindness. The law of love teaches us not to pray for an hour every morning and then go out in public and be rude to a salesclerk who doesn't move as quickly as we would like. When we live under the law of love, we will not give our offerings each Sunday at church and then leave the service criticizing the pastor. People who are legalistic are usually harsh with others who don't do what they do. Jesus was very stern with the scribes and Pharisees of His day. They were sticklers for following all the rules, but they would not help other people. He said they put heavy loads that were hard to bear on people's shoulders and then would not lift a finger to help those people carry them (Matt. 23:4).

Personal Reflection

How can you regularly practice showing love to everyone you meet?

_____

_____

_____

_____

_____

_____

_____

_____

_____

_____

_____

The best description of love is the one Paul wrote in 1 Corinthians 13:1–8. In the first three verses, he mentions spiritual activities and gifts, such as speaking in tongues and having prophetic abilities, and says that those are worthless if the person who practices them does not have love. In verse 3, he says that even giving every bit of money a person has to help the poor or giving one's "body to be burned" gains nothing without love. Then, in verses 4–7, he defines love this way:

> Love endures with patience and serenity, love is kind and thoughtful, and is not jealous or envious; love does not brag and is not proud or arrogant. It is not rude; it is not self-seeking, it is not provoked [nor overly sensitive and easily angered]; it does not take into account a wrong *endured*. It does not rejoice at injustice, but rejoices with the truth [when right and truth prevail]. Love bears all things [regardless of what comes], believes all things [looking for the best in each one], hopes all things [remaining steadfast during difficult times], endures all things [without weakening].

As believers, we are called to be loving and merciful. Mercy is kindness beyond anything anyone could possibly expect, and James 2:13 teaches that mercy triumphs over judgment. Mercy cannot be earned or deserved; it can only be given in love and received with gratitude.

CHAPTER 5

HOW TO HAVE A LIVING FAITH

Faith Without Works Is Dead

James 2:14–26

*What is the benefit, my fellow believers, if someone claims to have faith but has no [good] works [as evidence]? Can that [kind of] faith save him? [No, a mere claim of faith is not sufficient—genuine faith produces good works.] If a brother or sister is without [adequate] clothing and lacks [enough] food for each day, and one of you says to them, "Go in peace [with my blessing], [keep] warm and feed yourselves," but he does not give them the necessities for the body, what good does that do? So too, faith, if it does not have works [to back it up], is by itself dead [inoperative and ineffective]. But someone may say, "You [claim to] have faith and I have [good] works; show me your [alleged] faith without the works [if you can], and I will show you my faith by my works [that is, by what I do]." You believe that God is one; you do well [to believe that]. The demons also believe [that], and shudder and bristle [in awe-filled terror—they have seen His wrath]! But are you willing to recognize, you foolish [spiritually shallow] person, that faith without [good] works is useless? Was our father Abraham not [shown to be] justified by works [of obedience which expressed his faith] when he offered Isaac his son on the altar [as a sacrifice to God]? You see that [his] faith was working together with his works, and as a result of the works, his faith was completed [reaching its maturity when he expressed his faith through obedience]. And the Scripture was fulfilled which says, "A*BRAHAM BELIEVED *G*OD, AND THIS [faith] WAS CREDITED TO HIM [by God] AS RIGHTEOUSNESS and AS CONFORMITY TO *H*IS WILL," and he was called the friend of God. You see that a man (believer) is justified by works and not by faith alone [that is, by acts of obedience a born-again believer reveals his faith]. In the same way, was Rahab the prostitute not justified by works too, when she received the [Hebrew] spies as guests and protected them, and sent*

> *them away [to escape] by a different route? For just as the [human]*
> *body without the spirit is dead, so faith without works [of obedience] is*
> *also dead.*

In this second part of James 2, James urges us not to think we can have true faith without works of obedience. No one can see our faith or know that we are true believers if they don't see us doing good works. Those who have received Christ will demonstrate their faith by their works. A legalistic person follows rules and regulations hoping to get something from God by doing so. They may want admiration, favor, special privilege, or any number of things from Him. They are not doing good works by faith with right motives. Those who have true faith do good works and strive to please God in all things because they love Him, not in order to gain anything from Him. Faith comes first and then works. We might say that good works are the fruit, or proof, of true faith.

Unless it is understood properly, James 2:14–26 can be confusing when considered in light of Paul's teachings, which state that we are justified by faith alone and not by works. It's important to look closely at these verses, because we know that Paul writes repeatedly that we are saved through faith alone (Rom. 3:28; Gal. 2:16; Eph. 2:8–9). This means there is nothing we can ever do to earn God's love or our salvation. No amount of good works will cause God to love or accept us. Our relationship with Him is based entirely on the work that God has done for us, which we receive by faith.

Some people wonder if James is contradicting Paul when he writes in verse 17 that "faith, if it does not have works [to back it up], is by itself dead [inoperative and ineffective]." I don't think he is disagreeing with Paul at all. I think Paul is right, and James is right, too.

James is simply emphasizing the truth that if we have real faith, we will do works that prove it. By our good works, we can show people our faith, but we cannot show them our faith without good works. We may go to heaven when we die because of our faith, but without good works we will not have enjoyed our lives on earth and we will not have helped anyone else find eternal life. Good works validate our witness for Christ.

I like to say that we are justified before God by faith, and we are justified before other people by our works. Paul writes in 2 Corinthians 5:20 that believers are "ambassadors for Christ," meaning that we are the ones who represent Him to the world. How can anyone see our faith if there are no works to prove it? James is making the point that if we see someone in need and say to them, "Goodbye. Be warm and be filled," but we don't give them any clothing or food, what good does that do? (See James 2:15–16.) If we see someone struggling or in lack and have the ability to help them, should we simply demonstrate our faith by praying for them, or should we do good works and help them in a tangible way? Of course prayer is helpful and important, and if that is all we can do, then it is enough; but if we pray for God to help someone when we could help them ourselves, we are missing the fullness of God's assignment for us.

If all Christians lived their everyday lives in the world as obedient children of God, the churches would not be able to hold all of the people trying to get into them. Our good works would be like magnets, drawing people to the goodness and love of God.

When our love for God inspires us to be kind, helpful, and generous to others, they can see our faith, and we may get an opportunity to tell them about Jesus. If all we ever do is go to church, listen to Christian music, and watch sermons on television, people may recognize that we are interested in spiritual things, but they will not be touched, helped, or encouraged by our faith. If we want to have an impact on the world around us, we need both faith and good works.

Part of spiritual maturity is caring about people other than ourselves. As Christians, we all have a job—not just an office job or a teaching job or a job in a hospital, a bank, or a factory. Believers all have one job in common, in addition to the way we earn a living. Our job is to act like people who know and love God. It's to go out into the world and show people in practical ways that God loves and cares for them. It's to show the fruit of our faith by being kind, helpful, encouraging, supportive, and generous to the people around us.

Personal Reflection

What kinds of genuine good works can you do to demonstrate that you have faith in God through your personal relationship with Christ?

_____

_____

_____

_____

_____

_____

_____

_____

_____

_____

_____

In verses 19–20, James makes an interesting point about believing in God. We all know that believing in God is a good thing, but even demons believe. If we are unproductive and ineffective, our belief is worthless as far as helping others is concerned.

Look also at James 2:21–22. Abraham's belief in God was counted as righteousness with God, but it was not until he offered Isaac as proof of his faith that it was completed and reached its supreme expression (Genesis 22:1–19). He definitely had great faith. He has even been called the "Father of Faith," but God required even Abraham to affirm his faith with a work of obedience.

Not only will we fail to influence the world for God if we have faith without works, but we will also fail to reap the rewards that will be waiting for us in heaven based on how we live our lives on earth. I like to say that we need to spend our time *here* (meaning our lives in this world) getting ready for *there* (eternal life in heaven). When we do good works, we don't earn anything from God, but we do know we can expect Him to notice the ways we serve Him on earth and to reward us someday, because that is His promise.

Often, the fruit, or result, of a good work is that someone sees something different in us, something that makes them feel valuable, and it causes them to want to experience the faith that we have. That's when God can use us to lead others to Christ and give them the hope of spending eternity in heaven. It's amazing that we can be partners with God to make a difference in their eternal destiny! We don't always know who may see or benefit from our good works, but I believe that when we live according to God's Word and do what He tells us to do, there will be people in heaven who say to us, "I wouldn't be here if it wasn't for you!" We have no idea how powerful good works can be. If we want to make a difference in this world and be used by God to increase the population of heaven, let's do everything we can to demonstrate our faith through good works.

What do we say about someone who claims to believe in Jesus and to have faith, yet has no good works? All I know is that in John 21:15–17, three times Jesus asked Peter if he loved Him, and each time Peter answered that he did. Then Jesus replied, "Feed My sheep." To me, "Feed My sheep" means "Help somebody!" If we truly love Jesus, we *will* help others and show them His love.

As believers, our responsibility is to study and know God's Word, to grow in faith, to be obedient to God, and to do good works as the Holy Spirit leads us so we might accurately represent God to a lost world.

Personal Reflection

In your life, what is the difference between doing good works by faith and doing good works to impress others?

_____

_____

_____

_____

_____

_____

_____

_____

_____

_____

_____

_____

_____

_____

_____

_____

CHAPTER 6

•——⟨○⟩——•

FAITH AND THE POWER OF WORDS

James's epistle is about faith, and he helps us understand how our faith works in various practical situations. The faith that James writes about is a vital force that enables us to control a part of ourselves that can do great damage in our lives and to other people—the tongue. His primary message in the beginning of chapter 3 is that what we say makes a difference. Controlling the tongue and learning to use it for good, not evil, cannot be done without God's help, but it can be done.

People often use their words in ways that dishonor God and injure their fellow human beings. In fact, words are the underlying cause of most strife in the church and in the world. People also use words to inspire and encourage others, and words have been the basis for some of the great things that have happened in the world. Relationships can be built or destroyed because of words. Jobs and opportunities can be won or lost because of something someone says. The tongue is one of the tiniest members of the body, yet one of the most powerful. We will be wise to seriously consider what James writes about the tongue.

Every Believer Is a Teacher

James 3:1

Not many [of you] should become teachers [serving in an official teaching capacity], my brothers and sisters, for you know that we [who are teachers] will be judged by a higher standard [because we have assumed greater accountability and more condemnation if we teach incorrectly].

Sometimes people read this verse and skip over it because they think, *I'm not a pastor or a Bible teacher so it doesn't apply to me.* Although James is writing primarily to those in official teaching capacities, all believers are teachers in some way or another. As I wrote in the commentary on James 2 (see page 57), each and every Christian has a job to do, and that is to do good works that will show God's love and draw people to Him. If you are a parent, you are teaching your children. If you are a coach, you are teaching athletes. If you have a job and perhaps you are the only Christian in your workplace, you are teaching your co-workers, perhaps without realizing it.

As believers, we teach by example. We don't simply want to quote Bible verses, say spiritual things, or tell people we will pray for them; we want to show them with our lives how they can also know God's love and experience His presence personally.

Actually, we may do more harm than good if we say we are Christians but then fail to behave in a way that shows we are.

Personal Reflection

How can you live your daily life in a way that truly represents Christ-like behavior and attitudes?

_____

_____

_____

_____

_____

_____

_____

_____

_____

_____

The Power of the Tongue

James 3:2

*For we all stumble and sin in many ways. If anyone does not stumble
in what he says [never saying the wrong thing], he is a perfect man
[fully developed in character, without serious flaws], able to bridle his
whole body and rein in his entire nature [taming his human faults and
weaknesses].*

The only perfect person who ever lived is Jesus. Throughout the gospels
and in prophetic teachings about Him, we see that He used great wisdom
and restraint with His words. In John 14:30, Jesus was talking to His disciples and said, "I will no longer talk much with you, for the ruler of this
world is coming, and he has nothing in Me" (NKJV). I believe that, since
Jesus was about to begin His time of great suffering, He knew it would
be wise to say less, because when we are under pressure, we tend to say
things that are not helpful to us or to those around us. This shows us
that He knew when to stop talking, and that is a wise lesson for us to
learn, too.

Often, when we are offended or feel we are being treated wrongly, we
speak up for or defend ourselves. Isaiah wrote prophetically that Jesus
resisted this temptation: "He was oppressed and treated harshly, yet he
never said a word. He was led like a lamb to the slaughter. And as a sheep
is silent before the shearers, he did not open his mouth" (Isaiah 53:7 NLT).

In addition, Jesus never answered people who hurled accusations
against Him or made any effort to defend Himself to them. That would be
extremely difficult for most of us, but He did it. Luke 23:9–10 says that
the high priest "asked Jesus question after question, but Jesus refused to
answer. Meanwhile, the leading priests and the teachers of religious law
stood there shouting their accusations" (NLT). And Mark 14:60–61 says,

"Then the high priest stood up before them and asked Jesus, 'Are you not going to answer? What is this testimony that these men are bringing against you?' But Jesus remained silent and gave no answer" (NIV).

I want to remind you of James 1:19, which says, "Understand this, my beloved brothers and sisters. Let everyone be quick to hear [be a careful, thoughtful listener], slow to speak [a speaker of carefully chosen words

Personal Reflection

How do you respond to accusations?

_____

_____

_____

_____

_____

_____

_____

_____

_____

_____

_____

_____

and], slow to anger [patient, reflective, forgiving]." Jesus certainly was this way, and we would all be wise to follow His example and James's advice.

Being able to control what we say is a sign of spiritual maturity. If we don't offend with our speech, we are able to exercise self-control in other areas. Millions of people go on diets trying to control what goes into their mouths, but perhaps we should pay more attention to what comes out of them. Most of us would testify that there have been many times in our lives when we wish we had not said something we did say, because it caused a problem.

Small Things Make a Big Difference

James 3:3–6

Now if we put bits into the horses' mouths to make them obey us, we guide their whole body as well. And look at the ships. Even though they are so large and are driven by strong winds, they are still directed by a very small rudder wherever the impulse of the helmsman determines. In the same sense, the tongue is a small part of the body, and yet it boasts of great things. See [by comparison] how great a forest is set on fire by a small spark! And the tongue is [in a sense] a fire, the very world of injustice and unrighteousness; the tongue is set among our members as that which contaminates the entire body, and sets on fire the course of our life [the cycle of man's existence], and is itself set on fire by hell (Gehenna).

A tiny thing, such as a horse's bit or a ship's rudder, can make a huge difference. A large horse can weigh more than two thousand pounds, yet a bit—a tiny piece of metal in its mouth—can control its direction. Even a slight tug on the rein moves the bit, and when the horse feels that movement, it heads toward the direction the rider wants it to go.

Although all ships are different, an average ocean liner would weigh approximately 210,000 tons. The direction of that massive vessel is controlled by a small rudder being operated by a person at the helm of the ship. In the same way, the tongue is a tiny part of the human body, but it can determine the direction of our lives.

James also compares the tongue to a little spark that ignites a forest fire. We have seen from news reports that one little match thrown away carelessly, a campfire not properly extinguished, or a tiny spark can quickly become a fire that consumes millions of forest acres and even homes or businesses. Forest fires, like the tongue, are difficult to control, taking days or weeks to extinguish or contain, and often requiring firefighters from cities or states far away from the fire to come and help. If people would simply discipline themselves to use wisdom and common sense regarding matches and fires, most forest fires could be avoided. Just as a small spark can do great damage, so can one of the smallest parts of our bodies, the tongue.

James is teaching us in this passage that we can control what happens in many aspects of our lives by simply disciplining our mouths. The words we speak can give direction to our entire lives, and we will help ourselves immensely if we learn this lesson. Our words are powerful! Proverbs 18:20–21 says, "A man's stomach shall be satisfied from the fruit of his mouth; *from* the produce of his lips he shall be filled. Death and life *are* in the power of the tongue, and those who love it will eat its fruit" (NKJV).

Especially when we go through hard times in life, we need to be very careful about how we talk about our problems, trials, and tribulations. If we want to go through these situations victoriously, we need to speak positively, not negatively—to speak words of faith and not words of doubt, words of hope instead of words of despair.

Believers don't need to be the ones complaining in the workplace or saying, "Well, I hear the company is about to start laying off people, and I'm sure I'll lose my job." We don't need to speak negatively about what is happening in the world, in our churches, or in our families. No good comes from speaking badly about our lives by saying things like "Nothing good ever happens to me" or about our futures with words such as "I'll never amount to anything" or "My dreams will never come true." Instead, we need to believe what God's Word says about us, and then use our words to prove our faith and trust in Him.

We can and should choose to speak good things from the Word about what is presently happening in our lives and about the future. If we will receive God's grace to change the way we talk, it will affect our circumstances and change our lives.

Personal Reflection

What are some ways you can change the direction of your
life by changing your words? Think about specific sayings
or phrases you should change to reflect God's promises for
your life.

_____

_____

_____

_____

_____

_____

_____

_____

_____

_____

_____

_____

_____

_____

We Can Speak Blessings or Curses

James 3:8–12

But no one can tame the human tongue; it is a restless evil [undisciplined, unstable], full of deadly poison. With it we bless our Lord and Father, and with it we curse men, who have been made in the likeness of God. Out of the same mouth come both blessing and cursing. These things, my brothers, should not be this way [for we have a moral obligation to speak in a manner that reflects our fear of God and profound respect for His precepts]. Does a spring send out from the same opening both fresh and bitter water? Can a fig tree, my brothers, produce olives, or a grapevine produce figs? Nor can salt water produce fresh.

James 3:8 says it is impossible for anyone to tame the human tongue. Controlling our mouths requires help from God, and this means we need to pray about our speech often. In fact, I don't think we can expect to be able to control our tongues without devoting specific prayer and study to this subject on a regular basis. In Psalm 141:3, the psalmist prays: "Set a guard, O Lord, over my mouth; keep watch over the door of my lips" (NKJV). Psalm 19:14 says, "May the words of my mouth and the meditation of my heart be pleasing to you, O Lord, my rock and my redeemer" (NLT). You and I can pray these same prayers every day.

This passage from James 3 also teaches us that we can use our mouths for good purposes as well as bad ones. We can let God use our mouths, or we can let the devil use them.

I have studied the power of words for many years and taught about it often, yet I am still amazed that words can make such a difference in our own lives and in the lives of others. As James says, the same mouth can speak words of blessing and words of cursing. We can go to church on Sunday and praise God and turn around on Monday and gossip about a co-worker.

Learning not to speak negative and harmful words is very important. Words can do great damage to other people and to relationships. We would be wise to avoid hard, harsh, unjust words and what the Bible calls "malicious talk" (Isa. 58:9 NIV). Because when we say something hurtful, we can apologize, but we can never take it back, so we should be very careful about what we say.

Learning not to speak the wrong kinds of words is definitely good, but it's only the first step in controlling the tongue, and we need to go beyond that. We also need to discipline ourselves to speak positive, powerful words that line up with biblical principles. I have said many times, "The best way to keep from saying the wrong things is to keep our mouths full of the right things." I encourage you to form a habit of using your words to make people feel good about themselves. Let people know you appreciate them, say "thank you," and give them genuine compliments.

One of the best commitments we can make is to speak good, uplifting words. If we cannot do that in certain situations, it is often best to say nothing at all, as Proverbs 17:28 teaches us: "Even fools are thought wise when they keep silent; with their mouths shut, they seem intelligent" (NLT).

We can use our words to lift people up and give them confidence or to tear them down. We can speak to them in ways that make them feel good about themselves or bad. Sometimes what may seem minor to us is just what someone needs to hear to have a good day. In contrast, though, careless or casually negative words can ruin someone's day. Let me encourage you to speak words filled with peace, joy, and hope. Realize that your words can powerfully impact other people, so say good things about them and to them.

Many people have been raised in environments like the one in which I was raised. For many years, they heard negative words from parents and family members, and maybe even schoolteachers or friends. They never heard anyone say anything that affirmed them or gave them hope for their future. I understand this completely. When God began to teach me about the power of words, knowing that my whole life could change if I changed my words filled me with hope. He led me to make a list of Scripture-based confessions. Not one of them was a reality in my life at that time, but I confessed them twice a day for a long time. Today, *every single one* of them is a reality for me.

Personal Reflection

How can you use your words to build people up instead of tearing them down?

_____

_____

_____

_____

_____

_____

_____

_____

_____

_____

_____

_____

The most powerful words you can speak are the words God speaks. I encourage you to spend some time in your Bible, finding promises and truths you can confess about yourself and your life. Or pick up a copy of my book *The Secret Power of Speaking God's Word*, which is full of Bible-based confessions that will change your life.

CHAPTER 7

BECOMING TRULY WISE

The Fruit of Wisdom

James 3:13–14

Who among you is wise and intelligent? Let him by his good conduct show his [good] deeds with the gentleness and humility of true wisdom. But if you have bitter jealousy and selfish ambition in your hearts, do not be arrogant, and [as a result] be in defiance of the truth.

True wisdom is to be sought after. It won't just come to us because we are Christians. It's something we have to be diligent to seek, and it is more valuable than any other thing on earth. We learn from these two verses that people who are proud and haughty, or think they are better than others, do not possess wisdom.

Humility is a proper fruit of wisdom. People of true humility:

- know they are nothing without God.
- are quick to give God all the glory for their successes.
- don't think of themselves more highly than they ought.
- don't overestimate their abilities and underestimate the abilities and worth of others.
- are not quick to display their knowledge or give other people advice they do not want.

Personal Reflection

Does your conduct show the humility of true wisdom?

_____

_____

_____

_____

_____

_____

_____

_____

_____

_____

_____

Godly Wisdom

James 3:15–18

This [superficial] wisdom is not that which comes down from above, but is earthly (secular), natural (unspiritual), even demonic. For where jealousy and selfish ambition exist, there is disorder [unrest, rebellion] and every evil thing and morally degrading practice. But the wisdom from above is first pure [morally and spiritually undefiled], then peace-loving [courteous, considerate], gentle, reasonable [and willing to listen], full of compassion and good fruits. It is unwavering, without [self-righteous] hypocrisy [and self-serving guile]. And the seed whose fruit is righteousness (spiritual maturity) is sown in peace by those who make peace [by actively encouraging goodwill between individuals].

Human wisdom—what this passage calls "superficial," "earthly," "natural," "secular," and "unspiritual"—is very different from true wisdom, which is the wisdom that comes from above and is godly. If we allow our own minds to guide us without seeking the Holy Spirit to help us find godly wisdom, things will not go well for us.

When we consult our own thoughts and begin to think about situations in all kinds of ways, playing out scenarios in our minds and figuring out how to deal with them, we are reasoning. The Bible warns against mere reasoning. Proverbs 3:5–7 says: "Trust in the LORD with all your heart; do not depend on your own understanding. Seek his will in all you do, and he will show you which path to take. Don't be impressed with your own wisdom. Instead, fear the LORD and turn away from evil" (NLT). It is not wrong to think about a situation and look for a solution, but that should be done *with God*, rather than apart from Him.

When the devil told Eve in the Garden of Eden that God had lied to her when He instructed her not to eat from the tree in the middle (Genesis 3:1–7), it made sense to her mind, so she believed him. Her decision to reject what God said and embrace what the devil said caused trouble for the entire human race.

Romans 8:5–6 helps us understand the difference between the mind of the flesh, which represents human wisdom, and the mind of the Spirit, which represents godly wisdom: "Those who live according to the flesh have their minds set on what the flesh desires; but those who live in accordance with the Spirit have their minds set on what the Spirit desires. The mind governed by the flesh is death, but the mind governed by the Spirit is life and peace" (NIV).

Human wisdom tells us to get even with people who offend us, while godly wisdom teaches us to forgive. Human wisdom says we should save and hoard our money, keeping as much as we can for ourselves. But godly wisdom says we are to be generous to others, especially to the poor. Human wisdom urges us to stay away from our enemies, while godly wisdom wants us to be kind to them.

True Wisdom Is Not Jealous

James 3:16 indicates that there is no wisdom where there is jealousy and selfishness. James makes a very strong point about this, saying that jealousy and selfish ambition produce "disorder [unrest, rebellion] and every evil thing and morally degrading practice." No one wants to live this way. We need to take these words of caution very seriously, realizing that whenever we see jealousy and selfishness in ourselves or in a situation, wisdom is not there.

One of the most foolish things we can do is to be jealous of others. Being jealous of what somebody else has is futile because jealousy is never going to get you what they have. The only way we will get anything is to ask God for it and let Him give it to us in His own way and in His own time. To be selfish and jealous is not in accordance with God's Word and will lead to a life of contention, strife, and lack of peace. The wisdom that comes from God, on the other hand, results in blessing, joy, and peace.

Ask God for what you want, be content with what you have, and if and when the time is right God will give you more. If He doesn't give you what you asked for, He will give you something better.

True Wisdom Is Peace-Loving

True wisdom from above is always filled with good fruit. James 3:17 says the first fruit of true wisdom is pure, and then it is peace-loving. It does whatever is required to be peaceful and keep the peace.

Before Jesus ascended into heaven, He told His disciples that He would not be with them much longer (John 13:33). In John 14:27, He told them about a gift He wanted to leave with them: "My peace I give to you; not as the world gives do I give to you. Let not your heart be troubled, neither let it be afraid" (NKJV). Clearly, God wants us to live our lives in peace. We can see from this verse that while Jesus gives us peace, He also gives us a responsibility when He says, "Let not your heart be troubled." We can choose whether we allow ourselves to lose our peace or not. He wants us to deliberately decide not to let anything steal the peace He gives us. We cannot always control our circumstances, but with God's help we can control our responses to them, and we can choose peace.

One reason so many situations and relationships become stressful instead of peaceful is that someone says something they should not say— and it upsets other people. If we would simply learn to discipline our mouths, we would have a lot more peace.

First Peter 3:10–11 says: "For, 'Whoever would love life and see good days must keep their tongue from evil and their lips from deceitful speech. They must turn from evil and do good; they must seek peace and pursue it' " (NIV).

Notice how these verses agree with what James is saying in chapter 3 of his epistle. They summarize some of his key points in the chapter, especially that we need to be careful with our words and use them in a way that will promote peace.

Personal Reflection

How can you use your words to promote peace?

_____

_____

_____

_____

_____

_____

_____

_____

_____

_____

_____

_____

_____

_____

Peace is one of the most valuable, most powerful things you can have. It is connected to God's anointing (His power and presence in our lives) and His blessings. I have learned over the years that if I'm going to have peace, I must pursue it on purpose. The wisdom that comes from God does not merely desire peace but pursues it (Psalm 34:14). So the only way to have peace in your life is to intentionally go after it and to make whatever changes are necessary to your life, your thoughts, and your behavior.

H. A. Ironside wrote: "A wise man is a man of faith, a man subject to and taught of God. Such an one will manifest his true spiritual state by good behavior. His speech will be with meekness of wisdom" (H. A. Ironside, *James and 1 and 2 Peter: An Ironside Expository Commentary* [Grand Rapids, MI: Kregel Publications, 1947; repr. 2008], 30).

CHAPTER 8

EFFECTIVE PRAYER AND KEEPING GOD FIRST

James 4 is a rich chapter, full of practical advice about being a Christian. In the beginning, it helps us understand why we don't always get what we pray for and helps us know how to pray more effectively. Then it moves on to emphasize the importance of keeping God first in our lives. It also reminds us that we cannot change ourselves, but that God always makes "grace and more grace" available to us. It contains the familiar phrase "Resist the devil and he will flee," while also teaching us that being able to resist the enemy depends on being submitted to God. The chapter also reassures us that when we draw close to God, He draws close to us, and that if we humble ourselves in His presence, He will lift us up.

Why We Don't Have What We Ask For

James 4:1–3

What leads to [the unending] quarrels and conflicts among you? Do they not come from your [hedonistic] desires that wage war in your [bodily] members [fighting for control over you]? You are jealous and covet [what others have] and your lust goes unfulfilled; so you murder. You are envious and cannot obtain [the object of your envy]; so you fight and battle. You do not have because you do not ask [it of God]. You ask [God for something] and do not receive it, because you ask with wrong motives [out of selfishness or with an unrighteous agenda], so that [when you get what you want] you may spend it on your [hedonistic] desires.

I believe that James is saying in James 4:1–2 "You stay upset all the time because you try to get all the things you want through your own efforts. You are never going to get them that way. You will only end up being jealous, hating people, and having bad relationships because you want what others have." Then James summarizes the whole situation in one sentence: "You do not have because you do not ask [it of God]" (James 4:2).

Strife is a major problem in our lives. Not only does it steal our peace, but it opens a door for the enemy in our lives. God calls us to unity and lets us know in several places in His Word that if we are makers and maintainers of peace, He considers it a sign of spiritual maturity and it releases more of His power in our lives. I strongly urge you to do all that you possibly can to keep strife out of your life. Strife is bickering, arguing, or heated disagreement. We can disagree, but we must learn to do it respectfully and agreeably.

In order to keep strife out of our lives, we must love peace and truly understand the power of it. Satan works tirelessly to keep us in turmoil and we should pay close attention to what James is saying about how strife gets in.

Personal Reflection

Think about a time when you tried to get something for yourself instead of simply asking God for it and trusting Him to provide it. How did you go about it, and how did the situation work out?

_____

_____

_____

_____

_____

_____

_____

_____

_____

_____

_____

If we ask God for something and He does not give it to us, the reason is not that He is holding out on us. It may be that it is not His will or that the timing in our lives is not right. It may also be that there is something better He wants to give us, but we are not yet spiritually mature enough to have it. Whatever the reason, it is never because He does not want us to be blessed.

Many people use manipulation and worldly ways to get things they have no business having—and those very things end up ruining them. I have discovered that the secret of being content is to ask God for what I want and to rest in the knowledge that if it is right, He will bring it to pass at the right time. If it is not right, He will do something much better than what I asked for.

The reasons behind what we do and what we ask for are very important. God wants our motives to be pure, not selfish. Our work for God must be done out of pure motives, otherwise we lose our reward (Matthew 6:1–2). Being honest with ourselves about why we do what we do requires spiritual maturity. Anytime I teach on motives, the room usually gets very quiet, and I think it's because we are so busy "doing" that we don't always take the time to ask ourselves *why* we are doing things. Our actions should always be done because we believe God is leading us to do them or because we know they will be a blessing to someone.

It is definitely not wrong to ask for what we want, but let's make sure our requests are not based on greed or mere selfishness. We can be assured that God will meet all of our valid needs.

Keep God First

James 4:4

You adulteresses [disloyal sinners—flirting with the world and breaking your vow to God]! Do you not know that being the world's friend [that is, loving the things of the world] is being God's enemy? So whoever chooses to be a friend of the world makes himself an enemy of God.

Although this verse uses the word *adulteresses*, it is referring to anyone who forsakes God or turns their back on Him. Keeping God first in our lives is something we should work toward on a regular basis. The point of this verse is that we should never make the mistake of asking God to give us something that, once we receive it, will take us away from Him—for example, a career we have always wanted, a ministry, a family, a business, or any of the pleasures that the world offers.

Keeping God first does not mean we can't enjoy anything that is not spiritual or have other interests, but it means God needs to be first. That means He needs to be first in everything we do. First in our time, first in our conversation, first in our thoughts, first in our finances, and first in every decision we make. If we keep God first, then He will always take care of us.

The instruction to keep God first is so important that we can find it in several places throughout God's Word:

- Psalm 37:4: "Delight yourself also in the LORD, and He shall give you the desires of your heart" (NKJV).
- Proverbs 3:6: "Seek his will in all you do, and he will show you which path to take" (NLT).

- Matthew 6:33: "But seek first the kingdom of God and His righteousness, and all these things shall be added to you" (NKJV).
- 1 John 5:21: "Dear children, keep away from anything that might take God's place in your hearts" (NLT).

Let me say again that James 4:4 is not telling us we cannot enjoy being in the world or enjoy good things that the world offers. But we need to acknowledge God in all things and make an effort to keep Him first at all times. All Christians face temptation in this area, so it's something we need to work at and do on purpose. Many things in our lives compete for first place and attempt to crowd out God. Our jobs, relationships, the things we enjoy—all of these could take the place that belongs only to God *if we let them.* That's why James 4:4 compares loving the world too much to breaking a marriage vow to God.

The idea of a marriage vow between God and His people is interesting. You see, God considers us His wife. Whether a person is male or female, all believers are referred to as the bride of Christ. We are married to God. One point I like to make about this is that, just as a wife will often take her husband's name, God gives us the name of Jesus, which is "the name which is above every name" (Phil. 2:9 NKJV).

I have had Dave's name for many years, but I did not get it until I married him. I did not get his name while we were just dating. I often tell people that the only way to enjoy the privileges that come with Jesus' name is to move beyond a casual relationship and become fully committed.

Jesus' name is powerful! Philippians 2:10–11 says, "At the name of Jesus every knee should bow, in heaven and on earth and under the earth, and every tongue acknowledge that Jesus Christ is Lord, to the glory of God the Father" (NIV). When we pray in that name, we are presenting to the Father all that Jesus is, and those prayers will be answered in God's timing if they line up with the Word and will of God—as long as we keep our marriage vow to God. We have to keep Him first in our lives.

Sometimes people turn to God only when they face an emergency or a crisis. That's not keeping Him first. We should realize that unless God helps us in all things, we will be utter and complete failures, so the truth is we are desperate for God all the time, whether we realize it or not. If we seek God as if we are desperate for Him, we will find ourselves in desperate situations less often. We *always* need God! The more we realize that, the more attention we will pay to Him.

God is never more than one thought away from you. If you want to experience more of God in your life, think about Him and talk to Him. You don't have to use certain words or sit in a certain posture to pray; you just have to speak with Him from your heart. Remember, He wants to be involved in every aspect of your life. There is nothing about you that God is not interested in.

One of the best ways I know to keep God first in your life is to have a continual conversation with Him. Talk to Him and listen to Him. He does not always speak back to us using words; sometimes He responds by giving us thoughts or ideas. He speaks to us in many ways, and the value of developing an intimate, personal, conversational relationship with Him is invaluable.

People who are too busy to spend time with God are spending too much time on things that do not add to their lives but take away from their lives. I have learned over the years that one of the quickest ways to open a door to the enemy is to start putting other things ahead of God. If we keep Him first, we help protect ourselves. But when we let other things take God's place or cause us to think He is not as important to us as He really is, the enemy sees that he can take advantage of us, and he does.

Being diligent in keeping a strong, close relationship with God and putting Him first can be challenging because of the other things that compete for your time and attention, but it is the best thing you can ever do, and it will have a positive impact on every area of your life. If you will prioritize your relationship with Him above everything else, you will be amazed at the good things that will result from it.

The reason Jesus died was to tear down the veil that separated us and God (Matt. 27:51)—to make it possible for us to enter into God's presence and have a personal relationship with Him. He paid for our sins because God is holy and He cannot be in the presence of sin. So when we come to God through Jesus, He sees us through Jesus' blood—completely cleansed and clean. Because of what He did for us, we can freely go in and out of fellowship with God, and He can be a regular part of our everyday lives.

Personal Reflection

Is there anything in your life—a relationship, job, hobby, or other interest—that crowds God out of your daily schedule? If so, what changes do you need to make so that your relationship with God is your number-one priority?

_____

_____

_____

_____

_____

_____

_____

_____

_____

_____

_____

_____

As we think about keeping God first—before everything and everyone else in our lives—let's remember Matthew 22:35–39:

> One of them, an expert in the law, tested him with this question: "Teacher, which is the greatest commandment in the Law?" Jesus replied: " 'Love the Lord your God with all your heart and with all your soul and with all your mind.' This is the first and greatest commandment. And the second is like it: 'Love your neighbor as yourself.' " (NIV)

The Holy Spirit Lives in Us

James 4:5

Or do you think that the Scripture says to no purpose that the [human] spirit which He has made to dwell in us lusts with envy?

This verse says that envy is part of the human condition. But I want to point out that as believers, the Holy Spirit lives in us, and God makes us holy. We do not have to let our human thoughts or emotions determine our behavior. We are to allow the Spirit of God to guide us.

God is not sitting up in heaven waiting for us to try to get His attention. When Jesus ascended to heaven, He sent the Holy Spirit to earth to represent Him and take His place (John 14:26). He now lives in everyone who is a believer in Christ, and whatever we do or wherever we go, He is with us. There's never a time or place where He is not with us. If we will remember this, it will have a positive impact on our thoughts, decisions, and actions.

These are some of the other verses that promise that God is always with us:

- "He has said, 'I WILL NEVER [under any circumstances] DESERT YOU [nor give you up nor leave you without support, nor will I in any degree leave you helpless], NOR WILL I FORSAKE *or* LET YOU DOWN OR RELAX MY HOLD ON YOU [assuredly not]!'" (Heb. 13:5).
- "Have I not commanded you? Be strong and of good courage; do not be afraid, nor be dismayed, for the LORD your God *is* with you wherever you go" (Josh. 1:9 NKJV).
- "The Lord appeared from of old to me [Israel], saying, Yes, I have loved you with an everlasting love; therefore

with loving-kindness have I drawn you *and* continued My faithfulness to you" (Jer. 31:3 AMPC).

- "I can never escape from your Spirit! I can never get away from your presence! If I go up to heaven, you are there; if I go down to the grave, you are there. If I ride the wings of the morning, if I dwell by the farthest oceans, even there your hand will guide me, and your strength will support me. I could ask the darkness to hide me and the light around me to become night—but even in darkness I cannot hide from you" (Psalm 139:7–12 NLT).

CHAPTER 9

THE GRACE OF GOD

Grace, Grace, and More Grace

James 4:6–10

But He gives us more and more grace [through the power of the Holy Spirit to defy sin and live an obedient life that reflects both our faith and our gratitude for our salvation]. Therefore, it says, "GOD IS OPPOSED TO THE PROUD and HAUGHTY, BUT [continually] GIVES [the gift of] GRACE TO THE HUMBLE [who turn away from self-righteousness]." So submit to [the authority of] God. Resist the devil [stand firm against him] and he will flee from you. Come close to God [with a contrite heart] and He will come close to you. Wash your hands, you sinners; and purify your [unfaithful] hearts, you double-minded [people]. Be miserable and grieve and weep [over your sin]. Let your [foolish] laughter be turned to mourning and your [reckless] joy to gloom. Humble yourselves [with an attitude of repentance and insignificance] in the presence of the Lord, and He will exalt you [He will lift you up, He will give you purpose].

God gives us grace to overcome all the temptations and negative or evil tendencies in our lives so we can live in obedience to Him. The tendency to not keep God first in our lives is certainly evil, so we can count on the Holy Spirit to help us resist it. We may try and try to keep God first through human strength and self-determination, but we need God's grace if we want to do it effectively. Grace is God's undeserved favor and His power to help us do with ease what we cannot do with any amount of human effort.

God is always willing to help us and give us grace for everything we need, but we have to ask Him for it. People who are haughty believe they can do everything on their own, but the truth is that we cannot change ourselves without God's help. We certainly cannot change other people and we cannot always change our circumstances. When there is a work that needs to be done in us or in some part of our lives, we need God to do it. Our responsibility is to study the Word, especially in our areas of weakness, and to spend as much time with God as we possibly can. When we do our part, God moves on our behalf to do what only He can do.

The apostle Paul went through a situation when he wanted to change but found it impossible in his own strength. Romans 7:15–25 explains it like this:

> I do not understand what I do. For what I want to do I do not do, but what I hate I do. And if I do what I do not want to do, I agree that the law is good. As it is, it is no longer I myself who do it, but it is sin living in me. For I know that good itself does not dwell in me, that is, in my sinful nature. For I have the desire to do what is good, but I cannot carry it out. For I do not do the good I want to do, but the evil I do not want to do—this I keep on doing. Now if I do what I do not want to do, it is no longer I who do it, but it is sin living in me that does it. So I find this law at work: Although I want to do good, evil is right there with me. For in my inner being I delight in God's law; but I see another law at work in me, waging war against the law of my mind and making me a prisoner of the law of sin at work within me. What a wretched man I am! Who will rescue me from this body that is subject to death? Thanks be to God, who delivers me through Jesus Christ our Lord! So then, I myself in my mind am a slave to God's law, but in my sinful nature a slave to the law of sin. (NIV)

When I read this passage, it seems to me that Paul has worn himself out trying to change and become the person he believes God wants him to be. He's tried and tried, but he realizes he is powerless to change himself, just as we are. We are not able to live the Christian life in our own strength. Only Jesus can live it through us. We should do our part—studying God's Word, spending time with Him, praying, trusting God, staying in faith, and consistently doing what God asks us to do. But ultimately we need God's help and grace to be the people He desires us to be. I encourage you to develop the habit of leaning on God in all that you do, even things you may have done many times before and been very successful at. We need God's grace all the time in each thing we do.

Philippians 1:6 says that "He who has begun a good work in you will complete *it* until the day of Jesus Christ" (NKJV). *God* is the one doing a good work in us, and we can always count on "grace and more grace" as He works in our lives.

Vine's Complete Expository Dictionary of Old and New Testament Words says this about James 4:6: " 'But He giveth more grace' (Greek, 'a greater grace').... God will give you even 'a greater grace,' namely all that follows from humbleness and from turning away from the world." Our part in this is to make the decision to obey James 4:7 and humble ourselves, turn from the world, and submit to God's authority; His part is to provide the grace (His undeserved favor and the power of the Holy Spirit) to enable us to do it. The decision is ours; the power is God's.

James 4:7 is familiar to many people. When they quote this verse, they often say, "Resist the devil and he will flee," but they skip over the first part of it, which says, "So submit to [the authority of] God." While it is very important for us to know that we have an enemy and realize that he will flee if we resist him, it is just as important to realize that, according to this verse, our power over the enemy is found in being submissive to God. In fact, the more we walk in obedience to Him, the less the enemy can do to us. He may annoy or harass us, but if we are submitted to God, the enemy won't get very far with his schemes against us.

James 4:8 says that if we come close to God, He will come close to us. As I mentioned earlier, He is never more than one thought away. All we have to do to come close to God is think about Him or simply speak His name.

James 4:9 comes across as very dramatic, urging us to "be miserable and grieve and weep over" our sin, but this does not mean we should spend all of our time crying and thinking we are terrible. This verse is really a reminder that sin is very serious and an exhortation to take it seriously. Many of the things that are clearly sins in the Bible are no longer regarded as wrong. In the world today, some of those are called "lifestyle choices," "conditions," or "addictions." One of the biggest dangers Christians face is drifting away from the standards God has given us in His Word and toward the world's opinions and values. As believers, we cannot afford to think like the world thinks, talk like the world talks, act like the world acts, or believe like the world believes. We have something higher, and it is the Word of God. The Word is truth, and anything that disagrees with it is a lie.

Personal Reflection

Are you quick to repent when you realize you have sinned?

_____

_____

_____

_____

_____

_____

_____

_____

_____

_____

_____

_____

When we sin, we need to understand that it is serious and we need to sincerely repent. David was very close to God, but even he sinned. You can read his heartfelt feelings of repentance in Psalm 51. God is always eager to forgive our sin and restore us to right relationship with Him, but we need to acknowledge and confess our sin, repent, and ask for His forgiveness before we can receive it. Once we have done this He not only forgives the sin, but also forgets it (Hebrews 8:12).

In the amplification of James 4:10, there is a word that could cause some confusion. It says, "Humble yourselves [with an attitude of repentance and insignificance] in the presence of the Lord, and He will exalt you [He will lift you up, He will give you purpose]." It suggests we are to have an attitude of insignificance. God values us, and I don't think He wants us to think little of ourselves or to feel we are not important. At the same time, He doesn't want us to think more highly of ourselves than we should (Rom. 12:3). I think we should think and speak of ourselves as what I call an "Everything Nothing." This means we are nothing in ourselves, and we are everything in and through Christ; we have nothing without Him, and we have everything in Him.

If we will humble ourselves in the sight of the Lord and continue to pursue a personal relationship with Him, He will lift us up and give us victory in His perfect timing.

CHAPTER 10

AVOIDING WHAT'S WRONG, DOING WHAT'S RIGHT

Don't Judge Others Critically

James 4:11–12

Believers, do not speak against or slander one another. He who
speaks [self-righteously] against a brother or judges his brother
[hypocritically], speaks against the Law and judges the Law. If you
judge the Law, you are not a doer of the Law but a judge of it. There
is only one Lawgiver and Judge, the One who is able to save and to
destroy [the one God who has the absolute power of life and death]; but
who are you to [hypocritically or self-righteously] pass judgment on
your neighbor?

This passage contains a lot about the Law and judgment and even judging the Law, but it is basically saying that we should not speak critically against each other and that no human being can judge others because God is the only true judge.

When we judge people or use our words against them, we are not walking in love. If we would learn to live under the Royal Law of Love, we would fulfill the rest of God's laws. This is why the Bible says, "So in everything, do to others what you would have them do to you, for this sums up the Law and the Prophets" (Matt. 7:12 NIV).

In Matthew 7:1–2, Jesus gives us a clear warning against judging others: "Do not judge others, and you will not be judged. For you will be treated as you treat others. The standard you use in judging is the standard by which you will be judged" (NLT).

The tendency to be judgmental is part of human nature. Many of us can find things to criticize about other people more easily than we can find things to praise about them. Sometimes, no matter how many aspects of a situation are good, we can immediately spot the one thing that is wrong. Even though this is our natural inclination, it is not in agreement with the Word of God. So when we are tempted to judge, we need to resist the devil and ask the Holy Spirit to help us stand against temptation and to help us obey the Word.

In Romans 14:10–13, Paul writes:

> You, then, why do you judge your brother or sister? Or why do you treat them with contempt? For we will all stand before God's judgment seat. It is written: " 'As surely as I live,' says the Lord, 'every knee will bow before me; every tongue will acknowledge God.' " So then, each of us will give an account of ourselves to God. Therefore let us stop passing judgment on one another. Instead, make up your mind not to put any stumbling block or obstacle in the way of a brother or sister. (NIV)

In this passage Paul echoes Jesus' teaching in Matthew 7 and James's instruction in James 4, saying that we should not judge other people critically. Instead, we need to do everything we can do to keep our fellow believers from stumbling. We are each responsible for ourselves and for our actions. According to Romans 14:12, when Judgment Day comes, God is not going to ask us about anyone or anything except what we personally have done. He is not going to ask me why Dave did or didn't do something. He will ask me to give an account of what I have done, and nothing more.

Instead of judging other people, let's strive to be good ambassadors for Christ and good examples to everyone. If those around us are struggling with things, maybe we can help them or teach them something by being a good example for them instead of criticizing them.

Not judging others does not mean that we don't recognize sin or that we ignore sin when it is committed. We should recognize wrong behavior but respond by praying for the offenders and being merciful toward them as God is toward us, not by being critical or judgmental or by gossiping about them. There may be times when God wants us to go so far as to confront someone about wrong behavior, but even that should not be done with a wrong attitude but in love, keeping an attentive eye on ourselves lest we fall into the same sin.

Personal Reflection

Are you critical and judgmental toward people, or are you a good ambassador for Christ, showing them kindness and mercy?

_____

_____

_____

_____

_____

_____

_____

_____

_____

_____

_____

_____

_____

_____

Beware of Presumption

James 4:13–16

Come now [and pay attention to this], you who say, "Today or tomorrow we will go to such and such a city, and spend a year there and carry on our business and make a profit." Yet you do not know [the least thing] about what may happen in your life tomorrow. [What is secure in your life?] You are merely a vapor [like a puff of smoke or a wisp of steam from a cooking pot] that is visible for a little while and then vanishes [into thin air]. Instead you ought to say, "If the Lord wills, we will live and we will do this or that." But as it is, you boast [vainly] in your pretension and arrogance. All such boasting is evil.

James 4:13–16 describes people who are presumptuous and make assumptions about what they will do without consulting God. According to these verses, that way of thinking is pretentious and arrogant, even evil.

Presumption is not a word we hear often, but it seems to be a real problem in our society today. When we talk about it, we often use the word *entitlement*. It describes an attitude in which people think certain things are owed to them—such as opportunities, positions of influence, finances, preferential treatment, or exemption from rules other people have to obey. People who have this attitude don't want to work to earn things; they want things handed to them. This presumption is not pleasing to God.

I believe one of the things we need to think and speak a lot more often is "if God wills" or "if God approves." We really need to take seriously that God determines the success or failure of what we do, and we should respect and honor Him by seeking His will in all things and, as Proverbs

3:6 says, acknowledge Him in all of our ways. It's one more way we can put God first, as I wrote about earlier.

Often, we come up with plans and expect God to make them work, but people who are truly humble will always ask Him what they should do. They pray first, then plan. They don't assume they know what is right, and they will not presume upon the goodness of God or of other people. When we pray, we would be wise to include more statements such as "If it is Your will, Lord" or "God, if this is what You want for me." Mature believers realize that they don't always know what is best. Only God knows what is best, and we are nothing without Him.

One of the Bible's best examples of presumption is found in Numbers 14:40–45:

> Early the next morning they set out for the highest point in the hill country, saying, "Now we are ready to go up to the land the LORD promised. Surely we have sinned!" But Moses said, "Why are you disobeying the LORD's command? This will not succeed! Do not go up, because the LORD is not with you. You will be defeated by your enemies, for the Amalekites and the Canaanites will face you there. Because you have turned away from the LORD, he will not be with you and you will fall by the sword." Nevertheless, in their presumption they went up toward the highest point in the hill country, though neither Moses nor the ark of the LORD's covenant moved from the camp. Then the Amalekites and the Canaanites who lived in that hill country came down and attacked them and beat them down all the way to Hormah. (NIV)

There are other instances of presumption in the Bible:

- When the disciples presumed that Jesus did not want to be bothered by the little children who came to Him, they told the children to leave Him alone. But Jesus said, "Let the little children come to me, and do not hinder them, for the kingdom of heaven belongs to such as these" (Matt. 19:14 NIV).

- When Peter rebuked Jesus, saying He must not go to Jerusalem and suffer and die, Jesus recognized Peter's presumption and spoke strongly to him: "Get away from me, Satan! You are a dangerous trap to me. You are seeing things merely from a human point of view, not from God's" (Matt. 16:23 NLT).
- When Peter cut off the ear of the high priest's servant (John 18:10; Luke 22:50), Jesus put it back on and healed him (Luke 22:51).

We can all be tempted to be presumptuous, but as we grow spiritually, we learn not to put ourselves forward but to wait for God to do it. Jesus teaches about this in Luke 14:8–10:

When you are invited to a wedding feast, don't sit in the seat of honor. What if someone who is more distinguished than you has also been invited? The host will come and say, "Give this person your seat." Then you will be embarrassed, and you will have to take whatever seat is left at the foot of the table! Instead, take the lowest place at the foot of the table. Then when your host sees you, he will come and say, "Friend, we have a better place for you!" Then you will be honored in front of all the other guests. (NLT)

We are tempted to be presumptuous or put ourselves forward in various situations in our everyday lives. For example, sometimes...

- Young people with advanced degrees presume they should get better jobs and better pay than long-time employees who have worked hard for years and have the benefit of experience in their jobs.
- Athletes presume they should get playing time because their parents are friends with their coaches.
- Church members presume they should have the best parking spaces or be able to sit in the same seat each week because they have been members for many years or because they give large sums of money.

- Shoppers with just one or two items presume they should be able to jump in front of those with more things to purchase.
- Drivers presume they should be able to exceed the speed limit because they are in a hurry.

Personal Reflection

What's your approach to life? Do you pray first and ask God what He wants you to do—what His will is for you? Or do you make plans and then ask Him to do what you want Him to do?

_____

_____

_____

_____

_____

_____

_____

_____

_____

_____

_____

We all have to prove ourselves in life. If we will work hard, be faithful, and do a good job in everything we do, we will earn the right to have greater opportunities and responsibilities. In the end, God is the one who opens doors for us and promotes us when the time is right. We can always trust Him to put us where He wants us to be at just the right time.

Do What Is Right

James 4:17

So any person who knows what is right to do but does not do it, to him it is sin.

James 4 ends by teaching us that when we know what we should do and we don't do it, it is sinful. When we hear the Word of God, it teaches us something. When we learn from it, our responsibility to obey it increases. To not do what we know is right to do is as bad as doing something wrong that we know we should not do. Some refer to this as the "sin of omission." We can *commit* sin, but we can also *omit* doing what is right. Let's be sure that we are not merely hearers of the Word but doers of it.

CHAPTER 11

PRACTICAL ADVICE FOR BELIEVERS

A Warning Against Selfishness

James 5:1–6

Come [quickly] now, you rich [who lack true faith and hoard and misuse your resources], weep and howl over the miseries [the woes, the judgments] that are coming upon you. Your wealth has rotted and is ruined and your [fine] clothes have become moth-eaten. Your gold and silver are corroded, and their corrosion will be a witness against you and will consume your flesh like fire. You have stored up your treasure in the last days [when it will do you no good]. Look! The wages that you have [fraudulently] withheld from the laborers who have mowed your fields are crying out [against you for vengeance]; and the cries of the harvesters have come to the ears of the Lord of Sabaoth. On the earth you have lived luxuriously and abandoned yourselves to soft living and led a life of wanton pleasure [self-indulgence, self-gratification]; you have fattened your hearts in a day of slaughter. You have condemned and have put to death the righteous man; he offers you no resistance.

James issues a warning to people who focus on their wealth without regard for God or for other people. Being wealthy in and of itself is not wrong, but it is wrong to crave to be rich and ignore God in the pursuit of money. It is also wrong to use people to get more for ourselves and mistreat them in the process. The proper attitude toward money is that we should enjoy what God gives us but also be sure to give generously to the work of the ministry, to help people in need, and to do what we can to benefit others. The more we have, the more we can be a blessing. We should never let money turn us away from God, but always use it to serve and glorify Him.

Jesus says in Matthew 6:24, "No one can serve two masters. Either you will hate the one and love the other, or you will be devoted to the one and despise the other. You cannot serve both God and money" (NIV). He is not saying we cannot or should not *have* money. He is saying not to allow ourselves to *serve* money.

The only way I have found to successfully resist being selfish is to be aggressively generous and to be that way on purpose. My flesh frequently tells me what it wants. For example, when I take my daily morning walk, I hear thoughts like this: *What will I eat for dinner? When can I have another cup of coffee? What outfit can I wear that will make me look very thin?*

I hear a lot of "I want" statements from my flesh:

- "I want some new shoes."
- "I want dessert today."
- "I want to go out to lunch."
- "I want to rest."
- "I want to do something fun."

But Galatians 5:16 says we are not to allow our flesh to rule our lives. We are to be Spirit-led instead: "So I say, let the Holy Spirit guide your lives. Then you won't be doing what your sinful nature craves" (NLT). Our flesh will always have its desires, and temptation will come. But we can follow the Spirit and not obey the lusts or give in to temptation.

This passage also addresses people who have not treated their employees well. I believe that all Christians who have businesses or who have people working for them should treat their employees as they would want to be treated. They should not overwork and underpay people, but compensate them as they themselves would want to be compensated for that same job and offer fair working conditions, a pleasant work environment, and good benefits. Anyone in a position of authority represents the Lord, and they need to treat people well.

Personal Reflection

What is your attitude toward money? How do you use it to help others?

_____

_____

_____

_____

_____

_____

_____

_____

_____

_____

_____

_____

_____

_____

_____

_____

Wait Patiently

James 5:7–11

So wait patiently, brothers and sisters, until the coming of the Lord. The farmer waits [expectantly] for the precious harvest from the land, being patient about it, until it receives the early and late rains. You too, be patient; strengthen your hearts [keep them energized and firmly committed to God], because the coming of the Lord is near. Do not complain against one another, believers, so that you will not be judged [for it]. Look! The Judge is standing right at the door. As an example, brothers and sisters, of suffering and patience, take the prophets who spoke in the name of the Lord [as His messengers and representatives]. You know we call those blessed [happy, spiritually prosperous, favored by God] who were steadfast and endured [difficult circumstances]. You have heard of the patient endurance of Job and you have seen the Lord's outcome [how He richly blessed Job]. The Lord is full of compassion and is merciful.

James starts his epistle writing about patience, and here in the last chapter he writes about patience again. Patience is not just the ability to wait; it is the ability to keep a good attitude while we are waiting—not only waiting because we are forced to, but behaving well as we wait. It is also a fruit of the Spirit that can only be developed under trial. That is the reason God permits us to go through times of testing and difficulty instead of delivering us from them as quickly as we would like. God always has a plan for our deliverance, but He wants us to grow and stretch so we will be stronger when we come out of the trial.

James mentions the farmers who wait for their harvests, and we can learn a lot from them. He is saying to us, "While you're waiting, just keep doing what you know to do. A farmer waiting for a crop does that. He waters his seeds and pulls the weeds—over and over again, day after day. In a similar way, when we are waiting on God to bring something to pass for us, we keep doing what we know to do—praying, believing, spending time in the Word, fellowshipping with God, and being a blessing to other people. We continue doing these things while we wait—and we don't complain, according to James 5:9—knowing that God will move on our behalf when the time is right.

Personal Reflection

When you have to wait, do you wait with patience, hope, and confidence in God?

_____

_____

_____

_____

_____

_____

_____

_____

_____

_____

_____

Isaiah 40:31 is a well-known verse about waiting on the Lord: "But those who wait for the Lord [who expect, look for, and hope in Him] will gain new strength *and* renew their power; they will lift up their wings [and rise up close to God] like eagles [rising toward the sun]; they will run and not become weary, they will walk and not grow tired."

This verse teaches us that waiting on God is expecting, looking for, and hoping in Him. It is spending time with Him in His Word and in His presence. We do not worry while we wait on God; we do not get frustrated while we wait on God; we do not get upset while we wait on God. We rest in faith believing God will do what needs to be done for us at the right time.

Learning to wait with patience and hopeful expectation is a mark of spiritual maturity. When we find ourselves having to wait on something, we can patiently take a seat in Him and rest in God's presence. The promise of God's peace is not made to those who work and struggle in their own strength but to those who rest in Christ Jesus. As we wait on Him, our strength is renewed.

A Simple Yes, a Simple No

James 5:12

But above all, my fellow believers, do not swear, either by heaven or by earth or with any other oath; but let your yes be [a truthful] yes, and your no be [a truthful] no, so that you may not fall under judgment.

After we make a decision, we need to stand firm, letting our yes be a simple, truthful yes and our no be a simple, truthful no. I believe indecision and double-mindedness not only bring confusion and complication, but they also (as James 5:12 notes) cause feelings of judgment or condemnation. If we believe in our hearts that we should do something and then allow our heads to talk us out of it, we leave an open door for condemnation. We often labor over decisions when actually we just need to pray and then follow our hearts.

When we choose to let our yes be yes and no be no, we can make decisions without worrying about them. We do not have to live in fear of being wrong. If our hearts are right and we make a decision that is not in accordance with God's will, He will forgive us and get us back on course.

The Importance of Prayer

James 5:13–15

*Is anyone among you suffering? He must pray. Is anyone joyful? He is
to sing praises [to God]. Is anyone among you sick? He must call for the
elders (spiritual leaders) of the church and they are to pray over him,
anointing him with oil in the name of the Lord; and the prayer of faith
will restore the one who is sick, and the Lord will raise him up; and if he
has committed sins, he will be forgiven.*

These Scriptures make the importance of prayer very clear. They represent something I say often, which is that we should learn to "pray our way
through the day." In other words, we should pray about each thing that
comes up and not merely say prayers that ask for something. We should
also pray prayers in which we thank God for what He is doing. If you
have a need, pray, and if you're blessed, pray. If you or someone you know
needs forgiveness, pray, and forgiveness will come.

Prayer is not an obligation; it is our greatest privilege and one we
should make use of as often as possible.

Confessing Our Faults Leads to Healing

James 5:16

Therefore, confess your sins to one another [your false steps, your offenses], and pray for one another, that you may be healed and restored. The heartfelt and persistent prayer of a righteous man (believer) can accomplish much [when put into action and made effective by God—it is dynamic and can have tremendous power].

James 5:16 teaches us that confessing our faults to one another aids us in the process of healing and restoration. Many times we receive a release from what is troubling us when we finally tell someone else the things we have hidden, sometimes for years of our lives. Anything we feel we have to hide has power over us, but when things are exposed, the truth will make us free. We always need to use wisdom and be led by the Spirit when we choose a person in whom to confide. It is important to choose someone we know we can trust, someone who is understanding and will not judge us—a mature believer, who will keep our secrets and who will not be burdened or harmed by what we share or use it to hurt us or make us feel worse about ourselves.

We do not always need to confess every fault to someone else, but there are times when it is very helpful. I strongly encourage people to follow the biblical instruction to confess their faults to others when they need to in order to be healed and restored—but also to use wisdom.

James 5:16 says the prayer that can "accomplish much" is "heartfelt and persistent," which could be easy to misunderstand. We may think of prayer that is "heartfelt and persistent" as emotional and believe we have to "work up" some strong emotion before we pray if we want our prayers to be effective. For many years I believed this way, but now I believe that

James 5:16 means that our prayers must be truly sincere, coming out of our heart and not just our head.

Let's look at other translations of this verse that may make its meaning more clear: "effective, fervent prayer . . . avails much" (NKJV); "has great power and produces wonderful results" (NLT); "is powerful and effective" (NIV).

At times I experience a great deal of emotion in prayer. But more often than not I don't feel emotional. Believing prayer is not possible if we base the value of our prayers on feelings. I remember enjoying some prayer times when I felt God's presence, and then wondering what was wrong during the times when I didn't feel anything. I have learned to leave all that in God's hands and to pray by faith, not being overly concerned about what I do or don't feel.

We need to trust that our earnest, heartfelt, and persistent prayer is effective and can accomplish much, because our faith is in God, not in our ability to pray eloquently.

God Hears Our Prayers

James 5:17–18

Elijah was a man with a nature like ours [with the same physical, mental, and spiritual limitations and shortcomings], and he prayed intensely for it not to rain, and it did not rain on the earth for three years and six months. Then he prayed again, and the sky gave rain and the land produced its crops [as usual].

I like the fact that James makes the point that Elijah had a nature like ours. He was imperfect and displayed weaknesses, but God heard and answered his prayers. He will do the same thing for us. Don't let the devil convince you that God won't hear your prayers because you have sinned. We all sin and fall short of the glory of God (Rom. 3:23), but we all may be forgiven and restored through God's grace and mercy. When we repent of our sins, God forgives them and forgets them. To Him, it is as if we never did anything wrong and have a totally clean slate. We should learn to see ourselves the same way and boldly approach God's throne in prayer (Heb. 4:16), expecting Him to answer.

Personal Reflection

Do you believe that God will answer you when you pray?

_____

_____

_____

_____

_____

_____

_____

_____

_____

Help People Find the Right Way

James 5:19–20

*My brothers and sisters, if anyone among you strays from the truth
and falls into error and [another] one turns him back [to God], let the
[latter] one know that the one who has turned a sinner from the error
of his way will save that one's soul from death and cover a multitude of
sins [that is, obtain the pardon of the many sins committed by the one
who has been restored].*

Instead of criticizing people for their weaknesses and judging them for
their sins, we should work to turn them from the wrong way to the right
one. What an awesome power and privilege to be able to help turn people
to God and know they will be in heaven for eternity!

IN CONCLUSION

The epistle of James is very powerful, and it is filled with practical information for our everyday lives. I hope you have enjoyed studying it and that you will return to it again and again.

Take the time to consider each principle, and use them to examine your life and behavior, asking God to help you make any changes you realize you need to make in order to be in line with His desires for your life.

May you be blessed in your pursuit of a deeper life with God.

Do you have a real relationship with Jesus?

God loves you! He created you to be a special, unique, one-of-a-kind individual, and He has a specific purpose and plan for your life. And through a personal relationship with your Creator—God—you can discover a way of life that will truly satisfy your soul.

No matter who you are, what you've done, or where you are in your life right now, God's love and grace are greater than your sin—your mistakes. Jesus willingly gave His life so you can receive forgiveness from God and have new life in Him. He's just waiting for you to invite Him to be your Savior and Lord.

If you are ready to commit your life to Jesus and follow Him, all you have to do is ask Him to forgive your sins and give you a fresh start in the life you are meant to live. Begin by praying this prayer...

Lord Jesus, thank You for giving Your life for me and forgiving me of my sins so I can have a personal relationship with You. I am sincerely sorry for the mistakes I've made, and I know I need You to help me live right.

Your Word says in Romans 10:9, "If you declare with your mouth, 'Jesus is Lord,' and believe in your heart that God raised him from the dead, you will be saved" (NIV). I believe You are the Son of God and confess You as my Savior and Lord. Take me just as I am, and work in my heart, making me the person You want me to be. I want to live for You, Jesus, and I am so grateful that You are giving me a fresh start in my new life with You today.

I love You, Jesus!

It's so amazing to know that God loves us so much! He wants to have a deep, intimate relationship with us that grows every day as we spend time with Him in prayer and Bible study. And we want to encourage you in your new life in Christ.

Please visit joycemeyer.org/knowJesus to request Joyce's book *A New Way of Living*, which is our gift to you. We also have other free resources online to help you make progress in pursuing everything God has for you.

Congratulations on your fresh start in your life in Christ! We hope to hear from you soon.

ABOUT THE AUTHOR

JOYCE MEYER is one of the world's leading practical Bible teachers. A *New York Times* bestselling author, Joyce's books have helped millions of people find hope and restoration through Jesus Christ. Joyce's program *Enjoying Everyday Life* airs around the world on television, radio, and the internet. Through Joyce Meyer Ministries, Joyce teaches internationally on a number of topics with a particular focus on how the Word of God applies to our everyday lives. Her candid communication style allows her to share openly and practically about her experiences so others can apply what she has learned to their lives.

Joyce has authored more than one hundred books, which have been translated into more than one hundred languages, and over 65 million of her books have been distributed worldwide. Bestsellers include *Power Thoughts*; *The Confident Woman*; *Look Great, Feel Great*; *Starting Your Day Right*; *Ending Your Day Right*; *Approval Addiction*; *How to Hear from God*; *Beauty for Ashes*; and *Battlefield of the Mind*.

Joyce's passion to help hurting people is foundational to the vision of Hand of Hope, the missions arm of Joyce Meyer Ministries. Hand of Hope provides worldwide humanitarian outreaches such as feeding programs, medical care, orphanages, disaster response, human trafficking intervention and rehabilitation, and much more—always sharing the love and gospel of Christ.

JOYCE MEYER MINISTRIES

U.S. & FOREIGN OFFICE ADDRESSES

Joyce Meyer Ministries
P.O. Box 655
Fenton, MO 63026
USA
(636) 349-0303

Joyce Meyer Ministries—Canada
P.O. Box 7700
Vancouver, BC V6B 4E2
Canada
(800) 868 1002

Joyce Meyer Ministries—Australia
Locked Bag 77
Mansfield Delivery Centre
Queensland 4122
Australia
(07) 3349 1200

Joyce Meyer Ministries—England
P.O. Box 1549
Windsor SL4 1GT
United Kingdom
01753 831102

Joyce Meyer Ministries—South Africa
P.O. Box 5
Cape Town 8000
South Africa
(27) 21-701-1056

Other Books by Joyce Meyer

100 Ways to Simplify Your Life
20 Ways to Make Every Day Better*
21 Ways to Finding Peace and Happiness
Any Minute
Approval Addiction
The Approval Fix
The Battle Belongs to the Lord
Battlefield of the Mind*
Battlefield of the Mind for Kids
Battlefield of the Mind for Teens
Battlefield of the Mind Devotional
Be Anxious for Nothing*
Being the Person God Made You to Be
Beauty for Ashes
Change Your Words, Change Your Life
The Confident Mom
The Confident Woman
The Confident Woman Devotional
Do Yourself a Favor . . . Forgive
Eat the Cookie . . . Buy the Shoes
Eight Ways to Keep the Devil under Your Feet
Ending Your Day Right
Enjoying Where You Are on the Way to Where You Are Going
The Everyday Life Bible
Filled with the Spirit
Good Health, Good Life
Healing the Soul of a Woman*
Hearing from God Each Morning
How to Hear from God*
How to Succeed at Being Yourself

The Secret Power of Speaking God's Word
The Secrets of Spiritual Power
The Secret to True Happiness
Seize the Day*
Seven Things That Steal Your Joy
Start Your New Life Today
Starting Your Day Right
Straight Talk
Teenagers Are People Too!
Trusting God Day by Day
The Word, the Name, the Blood
Unshakeable Trust*
Woman to Woman
You Can Begin Again

Joyce Meyer Spanish Titles

20 Maneras de hacer que cada día sea major
(20 Ways to Make Every Day Better)
Aproveche su día (Seize the Day)
Belleza en Lugar de Cenizas (Beauty for Ashes)
Buena Salud, Buena Vida (Good Health, Good Life)
Cambia Tus Palabras, Cambia Tu Vida (Change Your Words, Change Your Life)
El Campo de Batalla de la Mente (Battlefield of the Mind)
Como Formar Buenos Habitos y Romper Malos Habitos (Making Good Habits,
Breaking Bad Habits)
Confianza inquebrantable (Unshakeable Trust)
La Conexión de la Mente (The Mind Connection)
Dios No Está Enojado Contigo (God Is Not Mad at You)
La Dosis de Aprobación (The Approval Fix)
Empezando Tu Día Bien (Starting Your Day Right)
Hazte Un Favor a Ti Mismo... Perdona (Do Yourself a Favor... Forgive)

Madre Segura de sí Misma (The Confident Mom)
Pensamientos de Poder (Power Thoughts)
Sanidad para el alma de una mujer (Healing the Soul of a Woman)
Sobrecarga (Overload)
Termina Bien tu Día (Ending Your Day Right)
Usted Puede Comenzar de Nuevo (You Can Begin Again)
Viva amando su vida (Living a Life You Love)
Viva Valientemente (Living Courageously)
* Study Guide available for this title

Books by Dave Meyer

Life Lines